THE NAME OF THE

ROOM

A HISTORY OF THE
BRITISH HOUSE & HOME

TONY RIVERS, DAN CRUICKSHANK,
GILLIAN DARLEY AND MARTIN PAWLEY

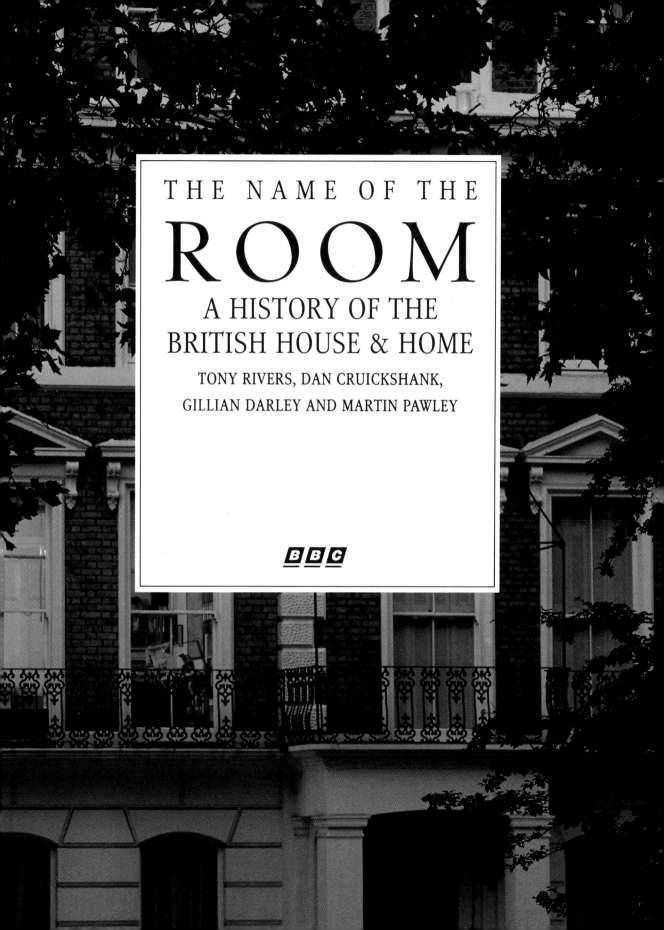

THE NAME OF THE

ROOM

A HISTORY OF THE
BRITISH HOUSE & HOME

TONY RIVERS, DAN CRUICKSHANK,
GILLIAN DARLEY AND MARTIN PAWLEY

BBC

Published by BBC Books,
a division of BBC Enterprises Limited,
Woodlands, 80 Wood Lane, London W12 0TT
First published 1992

© The Contributors 1992
The moral rights of the authors have been asserted

ISBN 0 563 36321 5

Designed by Harry Green
Illustrations by David Hoxley/Technical Art Services
Picture Research by Virginia Buswell

Set in 11½/14 Bembo by Butler & Tanner Ltd, Frome
Printed and bound in Great Britain by Butler & Tanner Ltd,
Frome
Colour separations by Technik Ltd, Berkhamsted
Jacket printed by Lawrence Allen Ltd, Weston-super-Mare

CONTENTS

Room in New York by Edward Hopper.
The poignancy of people observed in the rooms
they have made

CHAPTER ONE

HOME ENTERTAINMENT

TONY RIVERS

Darkest England

There is a brief time at dusk when rooms are lit and you can see, uninvited, into other people's lives. People observed in the rooms they have made have a peculiar poignancy. See how often they come and go attending to matters out of sight, transferring from room to room— those discreet boxes dedicated to aspects of living, those compartments of their lives. They lounge, eat, work, receive, cook, sleep, love, bathe, defecate, and each function, each zone within the home, is separated by breeze block partitions and thin doors, always closing.

British homes are the most secret places. They are sanctums, but also showcases. Within them are further graduations of privacy and territory. Their lineage is ancient and complex. Each contains memories of both much grander and more squalid habitations.

The front doors of the houses impress and defend. Their porches extend a qualified welcome. Their plump-breasted bays speak of openness and gen-erosity, but they are swathed in net for privacy and swagged for swank. Normally they are observation points. Soon the curtains will be drawn with a haste that speaks of guilt and reproach. Too much has been revealed to the voyeur and the indiscretion must be corrected. Or is tardy curtain drawing a tease, a partial display, the point of conflict between shame and show?

Admission to these citadels of homeliness is carefully controlled. A door policy is in operation. Judgements are made and rituals observed. When the door is opened the visitor will see nothing of the life of the house. The hall is arranged to screen rooms from public view and its staircase disappears into the darkness of an intensely private realm. A stranger or salesman will get no further than the door. Others will penetrate to the hall but will learn little more, for it is a zone of controlled decor containing nothing too personal. Some will be admitted further as the consequence of an invitation. Then there will be the ritual of welcome, coat-taking, submissive body language and only then the 'going through' to the living room, the penetralium.

Then the hall will be empty again, awaiting the next guests. This room is at its meanest a draught lobby, a home for a phone, a protected means of escape in case of fire, a corridor, insulation against strangers, mere circulation space, an intercession between rooms to render them all the more private. But its items of display—that vase seen only in passing, that mirror reflecting only the opposite wall, that table without purpose—are tokens of habitation, a recollection of the time when houses were halls and nothing else besides. With the rise and rise of privacy the hall has shrunk; it has been de-developed. It is the opposite of what it was. Now it is a barrier; once it was byre and bur, an expression of tribalism, of a lost communality.

The hall house in Britain was derived from the Anglo-Saxons whose culture supplanted that of a more sophisticated race in the fifth century. It was the habitat of a northern tribal culture. The Norman hall house was essentially similar but it grew. In its simplest form it was an aisled room with a high steeply pitched roof with a hole in it and a central flueless fireplace. Domestic architecture has always been a perishable commodity and perhaps that is why various published accounts of its development contain sweeping contradictions. Historical man seems to have had a learning difficulty, stumbling and fumbling down the centuries towards us. Inventions now seem belated and questions remain unanswered. Why did it take till the thirteenth century to invent (or re-invent) the wall chimney? Probably things worked just fine as they were. The central flueless fire of the hall house probably worked rather well because smoke rises as surely as water falls and the high ceiling of a hall was a sufficient reservoir for a body of smoke. (The smoke control systems of complicated modern atria are based on exactly the same principle.) There is also the fact that a central fire is more efficient than a fire on an outside wall and you can get twice as many people round it. The hall house may have contained the spirit of the campfire (literally housing a ritual) but probably, like much that bears on the history of the English house, it was just a matter of keeping warm.

That is not to say that the hall house would not have been hell to our modern sensibility. But the alternatives were worse. Only the fortunate lived in halls, the rest existed in turf hovels or dry wall huts. (The normal form of habitat in any age except for the present one has been the slum.) In the hall house men, women, children and animals were together. All the mess and drip and stink of life was there. Any daylight that came from the hole in the roof that served as a chimney would have filtered through perpetual smoke. In the dark and draughty slime pit below was the ultimate horror, the floor. Even in the fifteenth century the Renaissance scholar Erasmus was able to report thus on the condition of the English floor: 'Commonly of clay, strewed with rushes, under which lies unmolested an ancient collection of beer, grease, fragments, bones, spittle, excrement of dogs and cats and everything that is nasty'. Contemporary accounts refer to this early form of floor insulation as 'the marsh'.

But perhaps there was comfort and reassurance in the jumble and decay, the intimacy that binds the creature and his den, the closeness of the rotting

earth, the uniting stench. Since then the English have seldom risen far above the earth. It has been observed that they have wallpaper like tapestries and carpet patterns whose earthy splodges bear no resemblance to any geometric culture of pattern-making. They like to get back down home, go to earth where it is cosy, as in burrows, dens, safe havens. If this impulse is not folk memory it is certainly an idea rooted deep in English culture.

Mole tells Badger about what constitutes 'home' in *Wind in the Willows*:

'Once well underground' he said 'you know exactly where you are. Nothing can happen to you, and nothing can get to you. You're entirely your own master, and you don't have to consult anybody or mind what they say. Things go on all the same overhead, and you let 'em, and don't bother about 'em.'[1]

At one end of the typical twelfth century hall house was a raised stone dais upon which the dominant family ate. (A convention re-enacted in the college

A place where heroes might feast. The hall of Penhow Castle with its screen

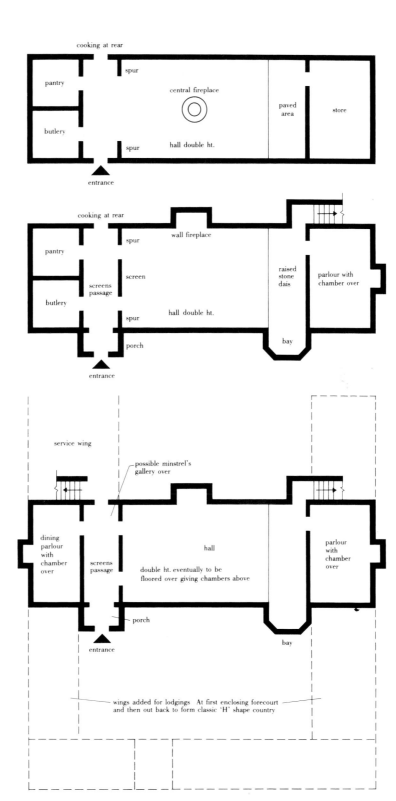

From hall house to your
house

halls of Merton & Magdalen.) At the other end of the hall doors were left open for the fire to burn. The resultant draught, which would particularly have afflicted those at the lower end of the tables, was mitigated by stub walls or spurs which perhaps also served to conceal the poor man at the door. Between those spurs there came to be placed a screen, an early room divider which would reappear as much else that is antique and deeply English in the houses of Lutyens (notably at Deanery Gardens) and oddly in modern houses of the 1950s. The resulting screens passage formed a vestibule and gave access to the rear where the cooking was done. Across the screens passage there came into being a 'pantry' (from the French for bread store) and a buttery (from 'butta', an Anglo-Latin word for cask).

The history of domestic architecture is largely the history of privacy and comfort, of the refining of sensibilities. It is also about money. The rich led the way out of the communality of the hall. They withdrew to rooms built adjacent to the dais, to—where else—withdrawing rooms. (A description later shortened and made specific.) The description might then have included a solar (a light airy room) and a parlour (from the French 'parler'—and meaning a room to talk in). Typically there was a parlour on the ground floor with a bedchamber above. During the thirteenth century, the parlour became the drawing room for the Lord and his family. Only in Elizabethan times, was it to become a formal room for conversation. This establishment of a private home life was condemned by the fourteenth century poet William Langland: 'The hall has come to a pretty pass when the lord and lady avoid it at mealtimes, dining every day in a private parlour to get away from the poor people.' One is reminded of a management consultant lamenting the British institution of the segregated executive canteen.

The hall house had therefore effectively become a hall with a one-up, one-down house attached. Then, at the other end of the hall above the pantry and buttery, another solar or bower was provided giving the form of a double-height central space with vestigial wings which, when travel became safer, would lengthen to provide lodgings for visitors. These lodgings were eventually extended to enclose a courtyard with a gatehouse before being cut back again to form the essential H-shaped great country house that would one day be filmed from helicopters in the service of the heritage industry.

The original parlour was in modern parlance 'a family room'. Another room was needed and the Tudor magnates moved the pantry and buttery to

Deanery Gardens, Sonning, 1901, by Sir Edwin
Lutyens. Great Hall and screen. Medieval
dreaming, deeply English

13 · HOME ENTERTAINMENT

the rear of the house to form a service wing with the kitchen. In their place they put a dining room, the third reception room and the hall became increasingly a place for entertainment and show. As part of this tendency towards civilisation, draught lobbies in the form of imposing porches were added to screens passages and (at the other end of the hall) prestigious bay windows were built. These displayed heraldic glass and windows like them would boast of bloodlines for generations to come.

> *The main hallway of the Sternwood place was two storeys high. Over the entrance doors, which would have let in a troop of Indian elephants, there was a broad stained-glass panel showing a knight in dark armour rescuing a lady who was tied to a tree and didn't have any clothes on but some very long and convenient hair.* From *The Big Sleep* by Raymond Chandler.[2]

There were now three display opportunities—the bay, the screen which became elaborately carved and the porch which carried additional self pro-motional information as to the pedigree and importance of the owner. His house was beginning to speak of money and power.

There remained just one addition to be made—a first floor over the hall. This required a wall-set fireplace and that was 'invented'. Early fireplaces were simple canopied affairs, a form which was to become a motif of the Arts & Crafts movements. By the fifteenth century the chimneypiece had attracted some wild and chaotic decoration, again of a heraldic nature. Such decoration, lacking a philosophical basis and a commensurate set of aesthetic rules, exhausts itself rapidly and founders in an over-elaboration which becomes a marvel in itself and a fitting testament to over-reaching pride.

The wall fireplace has ever since attracted decoration as the focus of a room (actually a tautology—'focus' is Latin for hearth or fireplace). Warmth of welcome and the desire to impress have made constant and often imcom-patible fireside companions.

Two further rooms appeared. A gallery over the screens passage for minstrels during the fourteenth century and a long passage in the newly created roof space connecting a string of chambers which is thought by some architectural historians to have been the prototypical Long Gallery.

Pre-Renaissance England is the period to which the English constantly return. It is the authentic 'olden times' re-remembered in the elaborate rural constructions of the Gothick revivalists and the Victorians. It is also recalled in ersatz medieval banquets during which late twentieth century clerical workers throw chicken bones over their shoulders in a belated contribution to the enduring English mulch. This rememberance of communality is of course a dream of a Merrie England that never quite was. We constantly perfect the past.

In terms of planning the disposition of rooms to form a house, medieval people were severe rationalists. Theirs was a natural functionalism as rigorous as that of any architect of the modern movement. There is a sense in which the natural development of English domestic architecture ceased in the sixteenth century. Our nostalgia for the golden age is perhaps prompted by a feeling of incompleteness. The asymmetrical, coincidentally picturesque nature of medieval houses is referred to architecturally again and again. It is in the joke-oak gables of semis, in the love of a steep and sheltering roof, the idyll of any country cottage, in the suburbs and garden cities, our connection with the earth, all that is rural and ideal in mullioned, wainscotted bowers and flowery doorways and lots of wood—the persisting idea of something sturdy and no-nonsense.

Here is Badger's home again:

It seemed a place where heroes could fitly feast after victory, where weary harvesters could line up in scores along the table and keep their Harvest Home with mirth and song, or where two or three friends of simple tastes could sit about as they pleased and eat and smoke and talk in comfort and contentment.[3]

The Italian connection

The Long Gallery,
Hardwick Hall,
1590–97. A room that
is its own view

The revolution which was the antithesis of that England came through the agency of Inigo Jones. Nine years younger than Shakespeare he spear-headed the invasion of Italian design that became for 200 years the fashionable architecture of this country. It is true that the sixteenth century house had already gradually become more symmetrical but Inigo Jones made it a beast of a different breed. From Jones onwards the thesis that theory precedes practice was ascendant. In other words that houses were *designed* and that the disposition of rooms could be subordinated to geometry. From now on there was artiface and there were architects. An innocence was lost.

The problem with the traditional hall-derived house was that its major features, the bay and porch, were asymmetrically disposed and (worse) the entrance was off-centre on the façade. Façades, you will note, had arrived. But there was a model solution. Whoever designed Hardwick Hall in Derbyshire between 1590 and 1597 took the radical step of turning the hall round and entering from the narrow end which was placed at the centre of the façade. Thus the hall changes both orientation and nature and takes a large step towards its modern meaning. The main room at Hardwick was the Long Gallery (166 feet of it) which contained some fancy Italianate decoration but which was lit by traditionally English mullioned windows. Equally significantly the Long Gallery was at first-floor level, on a *piano nobile*, an aristocratic level raised above the earth.

It is alleged by some historians that these rooms were for exercise in wet weather, but it is difficult to imagine the Long Gallery as a kind of proto-gym. It was quite obviously just a spectacular way of showing off. The immense perspective for one thing and then the rhythm of many windows, the high proportion of wall-to-floor space (all the better to display hangings) and the stately processional feel. The Long Gallery was to be a favoured architectural device of Adolf Hitler. It is a power promenade, the ultimate celebration of status, one way of getting your iconic vision of yourself in flattering perspective.

Inigo Jones's classicism was inspired by Palladio, the Italian Renaissance architect who revived and developed classical Roman architecture of the purest kind. English domestic architecture (which in this context means that of palaces) thereafter had to pass through the Baroque and the Roccoco

before it achieved a Palladian purity through the agency of Lord Burlington who revived Palladianism with a high moral intensity. It was Burlington and his architect William Kent who in 1734 took that giant step upward (the hall having become a virtual foyer) of placing the staircase within it. Early staircases had been of little account—spirals tucked into walls or simple straight flights. Even with the invention of the dog-leg staircase (not a major feat considering the more complex geometry of the earlier spiral stairs) and the inevitable addition of decoration, stairs had till then been consigned to separate staircase halls—examples of fine joinery and not much more.

Burlington and Kent's innovation happened at Holkham and it was a case

Making a progress out
of an arrival. The hall at
Holkham, Norfolk,
begun in 1734 by
Burlington and Kent

of the first time being the best time. It is said that Burlington derived the form of the Holkham hall from the Egyptian Hall of Vitruvius (a Roman architect of the first century BC whose theoretical work inspired Renaissance architects). The Egyptian Hall style was considered especially appropriate for festivals and entertainments. Holkham was triumphal.

So finally the staircase, the exceptional diagonal, had come into its own as a high point of drama in the house plan. A prestigious staircase needs to be wide beyond function. At its most showy it duplicates part or all of itself in a glorious redundancy, a conspicuous consumption of built space. It is the most expressive of architectural features. With wreathed handrails it can flow with grace or it can arrest you at each turn with stern newels. The Holkham staircase implies several people climbing abreast to somewhere important—the salons of the *piano nobile*. It transcends mere escalation and makes a progress out of an arrival. The grand staircase was to reach its apogee of showiness in the Victorian mansion, especially in those town residences and palaces of entertainment built for the London season. These were places in which to receive and be seen. Their staircases were for posing, decorative

Decorative lingering
and sweeping statements
in *Gone with the Wind*

lingering (imagine the confluence between the sweep of a stair and the flare of a ballgown).

Presently the chambers gave up their fair tenants one after another: each came out gaily and airily, with dress that gleamed lustrous through the dusk. For a moment they stood grouped together at the other extremity of the gallery, conversing in a key of sweet subdued vivacity: they then descended the staircase almost as noiselessly as a bright mist rolls down a hill. From *Jane Eyre* by Charlotte Brontë.[4]

Another consequence of the introduction of Palladio's super-intelligent Italianate architecture was the change in the relationships between rooms. They became for a while *en suite* in the continental manner. It was of course not unusual for English rooms to lead from one to another but never as an enfiladation quite like this, and never again. This wasn't just the absence of a corridor; this was a grand progress, a parade, shameless display.

In front and behind them walked guests dressed in similar ball-dresses and conversing in similarly subdued tones. The looking-glass on the staircase reflected ladies in white, blue and pink dresses, with diamonds and pearls on their bare arms and necks . . . All was mingled in one brilliant procession. From *War and Peace* by Leo Tolstoy.[5]

In the apartments of continentals doors are often in the centre of walls providing a promiscuous interconnection between rooms. The English soon put such matters to right. As the German diplomat Hermann Muthesius observed in 1901, English rooms were strictly segregated and English doors were not only located in the corners of rooms but were hung to open—not to the wall which would give immediate sight of the room—but to form a temporary spur giving the occupant an instant to prepare himself for invasion. In such ways the special quality of English privacy prevailed even in rooms on-limits to visitors. As late as the 1960s speculative builders would hang doors to obscure the sight of a room.

The Italian influence brought metaphorical as well as actual fresh air into the English house (another reason why doors were so hung was to marginalise draughts). The rooms of great houses became more public spaces, dedicated to entertainment. The segueing of shaped rooms—squares, ovals, octagons—implies not only a processional order but a perfection of behaviour and form, an enabling removal from the messier side of life. (Palladio wrote that 'rooms for baser uses should be hidden away as are the baser organs of the body'.)

These rooms for entertainment boasted systemised, intellectual decoration—mouldings, marbles, cornices, doorframes like sculpture, columns like monuments, plaster ceilings big and cold as ice-rinks. Everything was under control.

The English couldn't keep it up, of course, there on that rarefied *piano nobile* plateau. They took what they wanted from the continental model and gradually moved back and lower again, developing rooms which suited them literally down to the ground.

The English country mansion of whatever period has always represented the zenith of domestic fashion, technology and expenditure. These constructions were raised to impress and entertain. They were like great cruise liners moored in an ocean of fields. Aspects of their style, aesthetics and layout did however trickle down to the homes of the middle classes.

By the end of the fifteenth century, even some of the poor had dwellings of two rooms. The yeoman's house of the sixteenth century was like a scaled-down version of the great hall with an attached parlour, perhaps even with a parlour at each end of the hall. The hall was a combined living room, kitchen and dining room. Here is the origin of the farmhouse kitchen, another golden age dream redolent of goodness and nutritional values. The yeoman would eat at a gateleg table close to the fire at the family end of the room and his employees at a trestle table at the other end, just as once would the less favoured inhabitants of a large hall. The food would be cooked by the yeoman farmer's wife, a mythological creature from whom all culinary goodness springs. During the seventeenth century, the plan grew a little more elaborate with bedchambers accessed from a stair located within a small draught lobby of no pretension. As in the great halls, chamber floors were eventually carried across the hall. The result is a recognisably modern house form. Emily Brontë billeted Heathcliff in a variant of a yeoman's house built in 1500—where else could that earthy creature have resided?

> *One step brought us into the family sitting-room, without any introductory lobby or passage: they call it here 'the house' pre-eminently. It includes kitchen and parlour, generally; but I believe at Wuthering Heights the kitchen is forced to retreat altogether into another quarter.*
>
> *Above the chimney were sundry villainous old guns, and a couple of horse-pistols: and by way of ornament, three gaudily-painted canisters disposed along its ledge. The floor was of smooth white stone; the chairs, high-backed, primitive structures, painted green: one or two heavy black ones lurking in the shade. In an arch under the dresser reposed a huge liver-coloured bitch pointer, surrounded by a swarm of squealing puppies; and other dogs haunted other recesses.*[6]

It is evident that none of the above would suit in a Palladian house but classicism influenced small houses as well as large. The consequence has come to be called Georgian architecture. Georgian houses are almost literally chips off a larger block, fragments of Italian palaces. Often these were joined and the greatest of these aggregations were the terraces built on the hills of Bath.

(Thus it was that the topograph of that town and its terraced dwellings on hills gave name to any row of houses sharing party walls.) It is evident from Jane Austen that these ultra-modern new houses with their two first-floor interconnected drawing rooms were considered novel by refugees from great houses, but the upper class was quick to claim the new style.

> *She might not wonder, but she must sigh that her father should feel no degradation in his change; should see nothing to regret in the duties and dignity of the resident land-holder; should find so much to be vain of in the littleness of a town; and she must sigh, and smile, and wonder too, as Elizabeth threw open the folding-doors, and walked with exultation from one drawing-room to the other, boasting of their space, at the possibility of that woman, who had been mistress of Kellynch Hall, finding extent to be proud of between two walls, perhaps thirty feet asunder.*
> From *Persuasion* by Jane Austen.[7]

There were also, in the seventeenth and eighteenth centuries, architect-designed Georgian cottages, typically double-fronted and with a central staircase hall which gave access to two sets of double rooms. The double-room depth was facilitated by the Georgian double-span roof. Compared to the traditional one-room deep yeoman's house this was an innovation. In most Georgian terrace houses two rooms were arranged one in front of the other and further rooms stacked on top as required. Early eighteenth century farm cottages were arranged in a similar way, typically in pairs. Here is the embryonic early twentieth century semi-detached dwelling (Although the semi- is dressed in different clothes—spurning the sash window and all the trappings of classicism except the hipped roof, it refers to older models—the porch and the bay.)

Georgian houses, the product of the first speculative builders, attract enthusiasts who have inherited the moral intensity of Burlington, people for whom the past (specifically, that era of it) has a superior authenticity. At one extreme are the 'New Georgians', people who choose to live, as did the original Georgians, in places like Spitalfields and sometimes without electricity. They have become curators of their own homes. This is an interesting historical stunt in which the live roles, if they were not enacted by actual people, would have to be created by animatronics.

But generally Georgian became a style definition, a set of motifs which are thought to indicate class and a certain delicacy of taste. Its principal emblem, the sash window, introduced in the late seventeenth century, refers to high ceilings and enlightened civilisation. Upon its introduction, the humble casement came almost to be considered barbarous. The Neo-Georgian house of whatever period aspires to an imposing refinement. It is the style of money.

The small Victorian urban house, typically two rooms and a rear extension followed the two room-deep format but living took place on the ground floor which was divided into the formal front parlour and the rear room where the actual business of living was done—a separation which both preceded and outlived the Victorian age.

The front/back division has psychological soundness. It expresses physically the way most people behave, that is, they present a front to the world which conceals many aspects of what they actually are. That front must above all be socially acceptable, and respectability was a pre-eminent Victorian preoccupation. The front or 'best' room therefore had correctness as its first priority and could only express real personality within certain defined limits. 'Me' rooms had to wait till a more liberal age. It is however significant that, given the opportunity and the space, the modern house will incorporate a born-again rear parlour operating under an alias. Some old-timers retain front and rear parlours; indeed this is a room arrangement which suits the cultural customs of some ethnic groups. In that (and perhaps other senses as well) Muslims are the New Victorians. Those old-time front parlours do seem to hang around.

> *Mr Pietro Palermo was sitting in a room which, except for a mahogany roll-top desk, a sacred triptych in gilt frames and a large ebony and ivory crucifixion, looked exactly like a Victorian parlour. It contained a horseshoe sofa and chairs with carved mahogany frames and antimacassars of fine lace. There was an ormolu clock on the grey-green marble mantel, a grandfather clock ticking lazily in the corner, and some wax flowers under a glass dome on an oval table with a marble top and curved elegant legs. The carpet was thick and full of gentle sprays of flowers. There was even a cabinet for bric-a-brac and there was plenty of bric-a-brac in it, little cups in fine china, little figurines in glass and porcelain, odds and ends of ivory and dark rosewood, painted saucers, and early American set of swan salt-cellars, stuff like that.* From *The High Window* by Raymond Chandler.[8]

The Victorians purpose-built slums, their barracks of industry, their bourgeoisie ran braces of parlours but the *nouveaux riches* built wild mansions. It is a fact that the new rich will want to live in a house resembling those occupied by the old rich, but pure classicism seemed too dry a taste for the Victorians and their models were taken from some other golden age. They were far from the hall house mire, but they retained dreams of arcady. They revived the hall and transformed it into the rhetorical centrepiece of their concoctions (it proclaimed money and status) but their great mansions had many other rooms with specific functions or flavours to suit a complicated age. They included drawing rooms, morning rooms, dining rooms, breakfast

The Victorian parlour.
Here it is always Sunday
afternoon

rooms, libraries, sewing rooms, gun rooms, smoking rooms, closets, billiard rooms, conservatories. From these the modern speculative builder chooses names to designate rooms, not because the use of those rooms necessarily fits their description, but as an evocation of the past, a tribute to a continuing sentimental view of history. Function is secondary to the idea of how to live. Room names represent aspirations as perhaps they always have.

I equipped myself with a Music Room (I had not, at that time, yet learned to play the oboe), a Billiard Room (I had not, then, ever held a billiard cue in my hands), a Card Room (I was already fond of Rummy and Bezique), a Studio (in which I would begin my new career as a painter), a Study (in case Pearce should visit me and find himself discomforted by the oriental brilliance of my Withdrawing Room), a Morning Room (facing east, where I would sit between nine and ten to do my household accounts) and of course a most sumptuous Dining Room (the abundance of its table such that one would need to 'withdraw' a little after dinner to let the digestive system work in comfort and tranquillity). From *Restoration* by Rose Tremain.[9]

The Edwardians continued in the same vein. The most complete Edwardian houses are by Lutyens. The way the rooms are labelled on his drawings reveals the preoccupations of his time. Munstead had two halls, a book room and a Long(ish) gallery. Orchards had a hall, study, parlour and dining room. The fashion for male rooms is shown at Marshcourt which had a billiard room, drawing room, smoking room and gun room. (A ballroom was later added to redress the balance.) Lutyens's house plans were artful plays on medieval and Renaissance plan forms but it is significant that Lutyens the medievalist is more loved than Lutyens the classicist. Medievalism taps deeper roots.

English houses of this century turn between the Tudorbethan and Neo-Georgian modes. The battle of the styles continues. Each revival is more debased than the previous one but it is always sticks or bricks.

Crooked billets

The *Daily Mail Book of House Plans*[10] has been published for most of the last seventy years and illustrates, as proper architectural magazines do not, the aspirations of those who dream of dream-houses. It is a pattern book which has obviously changed in format, but its basic assumption that standard plans and types (that is to say, model houses) can be brought to reality and located anywhere, on any site, has not. The dream is so powerful that it over-rides locality. The consequence of a house that can be built anywhere is that anywhere becomes everywhere, a nightmare tract of dream homes. Like all dreams these are self-contained, self-generated and self-absorbed. Dream has come to mean aspiration or wish and where there are wishes there are fulfillers for them. It is in the interest of the volume house builders to promote the illusion that a house is a product that is not of the land, designed organically from its particular circumstances—that rise or fall in the ground, that tree, that view—but a product like any other to be manufactured and distributed, scattered, plonked down. But despite all that, indeed because of their insistence on disregarding physical circumstances, the houses illustrated have the force of icons. They show how the majority of people would wish to live in the perfect world of any particular year.

Tracing this social document through the decades is revealing. Standards drop steadily in terms of homogeneity and dignity of appearance. The earlier plans are more natural and straightforward, their space is worked less hard.

The area of each cottage illustrated in the *Ideal Workers Homes for 1919* is between 900 and 1000 square feet—approaching the typical 1100 square feet of a 1990s executive, four-bedroom estate house. The format of rooms for living in, however, is rigid. There is a parlour at the front and a room described as a living room at the rear. It is apparent that this egalitarian and neutral term has a proletarian provenance and perhaps that is why the reception rooms in 'housing' (as opposed to houses) are still designated thus. To the side of the living room is a scullery. Occasionally a hinged table flap is shown beneath the window of the living room (the yeoman farmer's gateleg table persists) and sometimes there is a dresser, an item of furniture which began life in the screens passage of a hall house. Stylistically, all the houses (semi-detached except for a few northern terraces) refer back to cottages.

The designs in the *Daily Mail Book of Bungalows*[11] of 1922 have a lightness

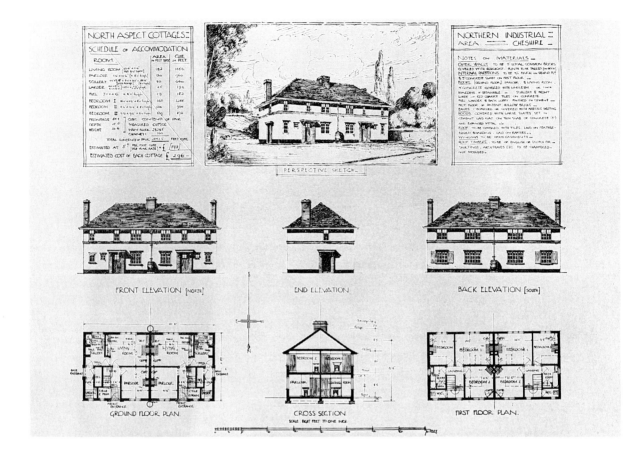

Demonstrating a socially correct and psychologically sound back/front room division, doors hung to screen rooms and the proletarian provenance of the living room

and elegance of planning which refer to classical archetypes. They are invariably 1500 square feet. Some are advertised as being of artistic appearance (nowadays this would probably be commercial suicide) and all are claimed to be labour saving. It is evident from the plans that the built-in labour saving device they all contain is a maid (even as late as 1939 there were one million domestic servants in Britain).

Instead of parlours they have drawing rooms and the formality of those rooms is often emphasised by their centrally placed doors. Instead of living rooms they have dining rooms and the dining room, normally shown with a table for six, is frequently the largest room in the house and *en suite* with the drawing room. In almost every case there is an additional service door to the dining room, giving access from the kitchen for the maid. She has a 'sitting room' indicating a perceived lower grade of sensibility. Some of the bungalows have a vestibule as well as a hall, the hall being a place of display. Sometimes the hall is as big as the dining room and sometimes it is separated by a screen. The word lounge creeps in, but only in a double-barrelled kind of way—lounge-halls mostly but also dining-lounges. There is no indication

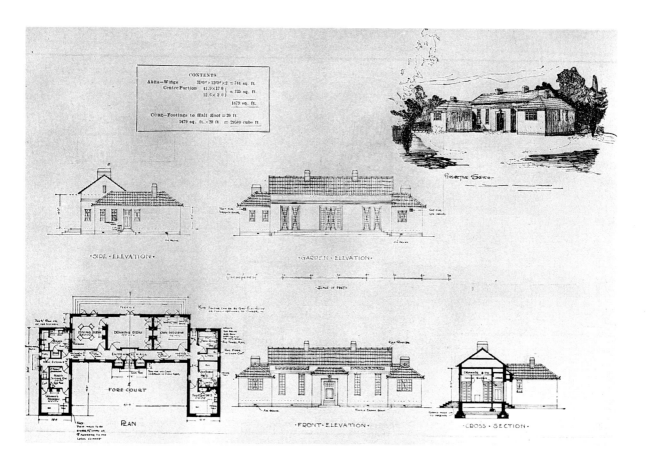

·SIDE·ELEVATION·

·GARDEN·ELEVATION·

·SCALE·OF·FEET·

FORE COURT

PLAN

·FRONT·ELEVATION·

·CROSS·SECTION·

A *Daily Mail* Ideal Homes Bungalow of 1922. An elegant and unforced plan, a vestigial courtyard and a hint of an earlier Britain

of rooms in which their middle-class owners could really let their hair down. Perhaps they didn't.

In stark grey contrast, in 1953 the *Daily Mail* illustrated plans produced by the Ministry of Housing. There was a timid approach to the open plan. Front rooms were now living rooms and positioned, logically enough, at the front of houses. They connected to rear dining rooms. There were bay windows and Tudorish fireplaces. There was an occasional dining space carved out of these houses of precisely 1000 square feet and there was the odd living/dining room and dining/kitchen. We can take it that this was an officially sanctioned view of what the postwar good life was to be.

By 1956 houses were getting adventurous. These houses longed to be free, to do away with dividing walls. Three decades after the beginning of modern architecture that aspect of its spirit had finally entered the English house. The architects of the Modern Movement wanted to abolish rooms—unhealthy and rigid boxes—altogether. They wanted free-flowing, omni-direction space within which there would be zones of activity. Walls and doors would be dissolved to produce a continuum of space and function—what came to be called open plan. Walls were seen as an impediment to the liberation of the spirit, devices of the bourgeoisie as bad as formal and restrictive clothing, worn-out relics of the whole of the buttoned-up past. The Modern Movement sought what in Palladio's terms could be regarded as the naked house.

The idea survives in occasional one-off houses built by architects for themselves (Michael Hopkins' house in Hampstead had rooms separated by venetian blinds) and in the shameless lofts of Docklands, wide open as the old hall houses. (The mother of one such loft dweller refused to visit until her daughter had a door put on the bathroom.) The anarchic plan dislocations of the architect Bofill (a living room contains a bath-tub shielded by a cinema screen) also cut through traditional shame/show divisions and are not entirely removed from the growing reality of jacuzzis, saunas and indoor swimming pools as public areas of the house.

The Fifties *Daily Mail* house didn't exactly produce house nudity or a Euclidiana for Modular man but there were attempts to break down the idea of the house as a configuration of boxes. To this end the chimney breast was often brought from the outside wall and used instead to divide living and dining areas. Screens returned between hall and living room. Sliding doors (then an emblem of modernity) formed a kind of movable screen. Dining recesses were in vogue but still with stub walls or spurs to mark them off from the living area. There were even split levels, and unsurprisingly the dining area was often on a dais. At around this time Americans had taken to building conversation pits (a concept really no stranger than that of a parlour). There were few conversation pits in Britain simply because you needed a very large room in which to set one, nevertheless the idea was around. That idea being of a slouchy, intimate area where you could really let it all hang loose.

The picture window, now in the 1990s a down-market item, was then new and prestigious. Builders were happy to advertise fireplaces as modern and open-tread staircases found their way into living rooms. So, in some extremely luxurious homes, did completely free-standing fireplaces with sculpted hoods and tubular flues rising to the ceiling. This was a terrific piece of showing off—a fire with the audacity to be not safely contained in a solid chimney breast surrounded by a kind of proscenium arch, but actually, dangerously, there in the middle of the room, its chimney floating above it. It was like an illusionist's trick. In retrospect the Fifties were a brave time. There was no weasel talk of traditional values, yet there lurked in the bright rooms of the model Fifties house the ghost of something ancient.

By the mid Sixties, the dream home had achieved the L-shaped room, the spurs to the dining room having vanished. There was an occasional TV room and just a hint of what would become a family room (née the 'living room',

Fifties audacity, open
and bright, but haunted

née the back parlour, née the original withdrawing room). Having established
the open plan, there was an almost immediate need in the ideal house for a
room to retreat to.

The new houses of the Fifties and Sixties were made possible by the
availability of economic central heating. One reason why the old front rooms
were seldom used was simply because it required too much labour to tend
two fireplaces. Central heating had two main consequences: rooms could be
opened up and there was no further need of a fireplace.

In the first warm flush of central heating, dividing walls were demolished
to achieve the new open-style, out-front living. Rooms intended as discreet
entities found themselves unnaturally conjoined. People couldn't stand the
thought of a room only occasionally visited and there were too many
memories of Sunday-afternoon rooms, Christmas-rooms with relations, best
behaviour in best rooms that smelt of cherished upholstery, furniture polish
and a hint of damp. People's sensibilities were knocked through, or so it
seemed.

Then there was the fitted carpet. At last a soft floor that, unlike the ancestral
floor of reeds, was also clean. It was the final touch, the last straw, soft and
yielding, to the Englishman's cocoon and ever since wall-to-wall carpet has
gone on and on throughout the great indoors. As for fireplaces, the Sixties
speculative builders thought that they could dispense with these costly anach-
ronisms which had long been reducing in size. They thought they could take
the hearth out of the home. Architects rejoiced in the idea of free-flowing
space without the tyranny of focus, the antique huddling together for

warmth. Every square foot of the house could now be of equal use and validity. They reckoned without folk-memory and the power of a symbol of survival, welcome and place. They lost the traditional and supreme opportunity for display.

Kerb appeal. The Cunningham by Barratt, 1991 'House of the Year'

> *. . . but the room had awakened in him a sort of nostalgia, a sort of ancestral memory. It seemed to him that he knew exactly what it felt like to sit in a room like this, in an armchair beside an open fire with your feet in the fender and a kettle on the hob; utterly alone, utterly secure, with nobody watching you, no voice pursuing you, no sound except the singing of the kettle and the friendly ticking of the clock.* From *1984* by George Orwell.[12]

The tide was turning again by the start of the Eighties. The big housebuying money was turning again to tradition. A new generation claimed a Georgian birthright and some of the rooms that went with it. House of the Year for 1981 was a stunted Georgian thing with a separate lounge and dining room and a morning/breakfast room. Stairs, having ventured briefly into living rooms, were firmly reconsigned to the hall.

We arrive at the culmination of a thousand years of English house development, at the 1991 House of the Year 'The Cunningham' by Barratt. Appropriately a collage of all our yesteryears, apparently the most desirable volume-produced house in Britain.

Houses are now, more than ever, marketed products with names redolent of prestigious places, bosky dells or popular history. Among this year's other award winners are The Savoy, The Sherwood Dene, The Englewood, The Brontë, The Queensbury, The Porchester, The Limegate, The Colonial, The Shelley, The Kipling. Tudorbethan houses get the leafier monicker; Georgian, the more pompous title. Cunningham is a bit of a puzzle. Impeccably English, it sounds like the name of a public school headmaster. The definite article is also important, if misleading. The Cunningham is intended by its manufacturer to be simply one of many *doppelgängers* beamed all over this island. Like any other product it is carefully costed and designed. It must have lots of extras just like a luxury car, and above all it must have kerb appeal so that the punter falls for it before he even gets out of his motor outside the show house. A lot of facade is important (it must have presence in its particular cul-de-sac) and one or two external features which catch in the memory just as surely as the hook line in a pop song. These features are part of a complex semiology but it is one that is universally understood. Unlike almost any other product, the new house must in some way seem old and new at the same time. It must be history without inconvenience. There is nothing particularly new in all this. Victorian magnates built medieval houses. What *is* extraordinary is the nominal and skimpy nature of historical reference. A single strip of dark stained timber nailed down the centre of a rendered gable (which has no real business being there anyway but is simply a symbolic excrescence of the main roof) evokes a millenium of English architectural history.

Having sent out all the right messages the house must have the correct complement of rooms but must also arrange those rooms with immense cunning for maximum utility and show. When every square foot you build costs £50 or so the discipline is immense. The draughtsmen or technicians who design these things (it is seldom an architect) have therefore developed considerable skill. Try to amend just one of these seemingly chaotic plans and the whole thing unravels before you. Their Rubic complexity would bewilder an early twentieth century house designer. Structure no longer affects layout. A few well-placed steel beams and a factory-made trussed roof give the designer a box to work within. The plans lack clarity and the kind of integrity that comes from structural logic but that doesn't matter. The whole concoction has nothing to do with any of that sort of thing. Externally, the box has bits clipped on to transmit the right messages and internally it is a warren of partitions so arranged to refer to other places, other rooms; it is

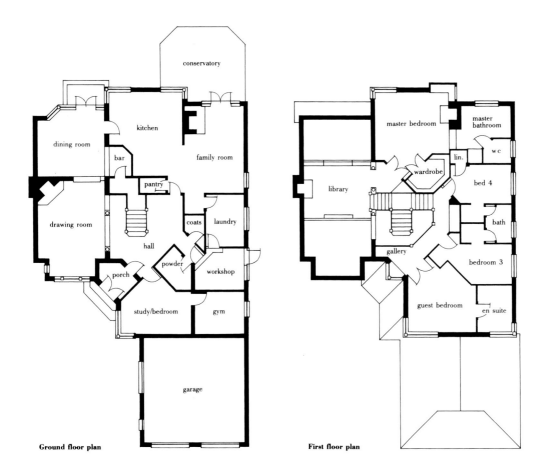

Ground floor plan

First floor plan

the art of the 8′ × 4′ plasterboard. It is also deeply post-modern in being referential, symbolic, iconic, image-stricken. The style, and indeed the spaces of the public areas, contain architectural non-sequitors but its so-called features are winners in their own right. It is like an album of opera highlights, the best of architectural history—all of it, a box of goodies.

Externally The Cunningham brags a brace of gables, a few hips and a couple of hip/gable amalgamations. There is something for everyone. On the garage doors the Tudor appliqué runs into a shallow arch. On the drawing room facade it turns a trick and becomes solid to form mullions dividing French windows in Victorian proportion. The single stained board tacked on over the Georgian front door demonstrates Tudorbethan symbolism in its purest form. Beside the front door is a gabled bay and elsewhere there are corner windows purloined from Modernism.

The front door is accessed from a porch and then there is a galleried stair hall containing a double flight newelled stair, classical in form but close to the spirit of those that Victorian barons used to impress visitors. The study

adjacent to the entrance, that might once have been called a business room, is there as though designed for the collection of rents from tenant farmers but in reality to write out cheques for electricity bills. There are spurs and a vestigial screen between the stair hall and the sunken drawing room (shades of the conversation pit). A debased fragment of an Inigo Jones plaster moulding leers wall-eyed back to the Renaissance and a reproduction Louis the Something fire surround is parked in a corner. You can tell that it's just an ornament because the room cannot be furnished in such a way that chairs can surround it. Priority is given to a shallow archway which affords access to the dining room.

All up-market speculative houses have dining rooms which are for occasional entertainment and full-time symbolism, just as were the old front parlours. The table at which you eat is the second primary indicator of home but, like the fireplace which is retained as a symbol, the dining table and the room that houses it is actually in decline. Changing work patterns, the diminishing family, the drift from formality, the TV dinner and the growing habit of grazing have reduced the importance of dining rooms. Regular use of a dining room now represents an unusual declaration for formality but, for a certain class, to possess one is a necessity.

> *His little dinners, in the setting of which Lord Henry always assisted him, were noted as much for the careful selection and placing of those invited, as for the exquisite taste shown in the decoration of the table, with its subtle symphonic arrangement of exotic flowers, and embroidered cloths, and antique plate of gold and silver.* From *The Portrait of Dorian Gray* by Oscar Wilde.[13]

Most eating now takes place in the kitchen which has absorbed the breakfast room and, in the case of The Cunningham, is a continuum with the family room. Family rooms are all the rage in executive homes, absorbing all the mess and drip of family life and liberating the drawing room for display. The Cunningham conservatory is off the family room. Usually conservatories are clipped on to dining rooms because the modern conservatory, unlike the Victorian version which was a summer room and winter garden, is in the nature of a glass display case.

The double stairs only affect a glorious redundancy. One leg goes to secondary bedrooms, the other to a gallery which gives access to the master bedroom. The gallery bestrides the drawing and dining rooms and gives a minstrel's gallery effect to each. It is described as a library but there is very little wall space for books. It is in fact a semi-private withdrawing room for the lord and his lady who might wish to remove themselves, not from the poor but from their children.

Most of the above can be seen from a point just inside the entrance hall. This is not just for the astonishment of guests. It was intended first for the benefit of the potential purchaser to reinforce his kerbside impressions; he must get that certain feeling.

> *... and we saw—ah! it was beautiful—a splendid place carpeted with crimson, and crimson-covered chairs and tables, and a pure white ceiling bordered by gold, a shower of glass-drops hanging in silver chains from the centres, and shimmering with little soft tapers.* From *Wuthering Heights* by Emily Brontë.[14]

Perhaps not in this particular house (it's big enough to take care of itself) but in smaller ones the internal doors would have been removed and the lights left full on to give a misleading impression of light and space. Spec-built houses are eternal touts, their own salesrooms.

The Cunningham illustrates history viewed as a swatch of architectural features. If the history of architecture were copyrightable this house would be arrested for plagiarism. But for all its ghosts and echoes it demonstrates a kind of cultural disenfranchisement, a deracination. The Cunningham and

Swanky stairs and a modest library

other houses like it, are basically the homes of the *nouveaux riches*. Its architectural disjunctions are cunning but artless and override the organic development of the English house. Its display is contrived. It has the thinness of image which can be detected in most modern reception rooms. An important thread seems to have broken. There is an absence of a strong solid room culture and that is particularly true of working-class living rooms.

Class structures and room domination

Richard Hoggart wrote *The Uses of Literacy* in the mid 1950s. Even as late as then, he was able to chronicle a homogeneous working-class life which now seems impossibly remote. He observed that sin was any act against the integrity of home. The worst thing you could be was a home-breaker. (And quite naturally, because traditionally a broken home could lead to the workhouse which was no house at all.) Therefore the home, at its most basic the living room and hearth, was more than a product, more than just your single greatest purchase; it was sacred, inviolable.

According to Hoggart, the working-class girl had an innate ability to assemble a home:

> *Watch the way a girl who, in view of the extent to which her taste is assaulted by the flashy and trivial, should have an appalling sense of style, can impose on even the individually ugly items she buys that sense of what it is important to create in a living room.*[15]

Some items were home-made, that is *really* home-made, not the conveniences of the DIY industry. In front of her hearth there might have been a 'clip rug'. The clip rug was a piece of hessian to which small pieces of cloth were sewn. The cloth was cut-up suits, skirts, any material which came to hand. Having assembled your palette of clips you could create a unique personal design that lay at the centre of the home. Clip rugs were not carriers of status. They were emblems of homeliness, a complement to the talismanic hearth.

A working-class living room 1946

A working-class living room 1991

However, Hoggart (always the romantic puritan) noted that when the age of utility ended the working class rushed to buy shiny new chainstore furniture. In terms of consumables there was a lot of catching up to do. The catching up has been going on now for more than a generation and there has never been a time when so large a proportion of the population has been formed by the *nouveaux riches*. The result has been a riot of what the visually educated would consider bad taste but the fact that affluence permits the acquisition of more and more ugliness is less important than the fact that the bought-in objects do not represent any real continuation of a tradition. The enduring working-class notion that decorative elaboration *is* beauty (not dissimilar to that of the medieval lord whose screen was whittled to the point of extinction) has resulted in a kind of tinsel Baroque. This phenomenon includes references to the past (someone else's). Sartre wrote: 'The past is a luxury reserved for the rich'. That was true at the time but is so no longer. The past has gone down-market. Its celebration by the newly affluent is not just for the sake of appropriating an (apparent) tradition but has happened because, as everybody knows, the past is more ornamental than the present.

It is striking to see how the modern equivalent of Hoggart's girl will use ornaments and decoration to feminise her living room. In this women's realm lacy curtains flounce and billow like wedding gowns. Decorative place mats and coasters intervene chastely. Family photographs substitute for ancestral portraits but with the curious inversion that the photographs are seldom of predecessors and almost always of progeny. Look at what I have produced, they say, see my position at the centre of my family. And then there are the pictures of cherished moments, the wedding photographs which seem to be the founding document of the household. All is soft and sweet, but it is not the natural habitat of the hulking brute crawling back to his billet. Men occupying such rooms can look ridiculous; they wouldn't dream of wearing frills but they will live in a condition of decor transvestism. Can they really feel at home or are they perpetual guests, their behaviour circumscribed and tamed by these feathered nests?

Perhaps this is why dens are becoming popular, especially in the bungalows of Essex. Dens assert masculinity. The name is evocative of musky lays, foxy hides. The den is distantly related to the library, the after-dinner dining room, the clergyman's study, the business room of a great house, the male dressing room, the gun room, the smoking room, the billiard room. In its suggestion of earth floors and rushes it recalls the ancient mire. It is a special kind of

withdrawing room—from the sensory deprivation, the anti-resistance, the fleshy give of the new foamy heaven.

Comfort is modern. Fifty years after Jane Austen's death, her nephew E. Austen Leigh chronicled the austere circumstances of his parents generation:

> ... *There would often be but one sofa in the house and that a stiff, angular, uncomfortable article. There were no deep easy-chairs, nor other appliances for lounging; for to lie down, or even to lean back, was a luxury permitted only to old persons or invalids.*[16]

But even E. Austen Leigh, the relatively comfortable Victorian, missed out on laminated foam, the whole science of ergonomics and decor sensuality.

> ... *there was a thick pinkish Chinese rug in which a gopher could have spent a week without showing his nose above the nap. There were floor cushions, bits of old silk tossed around, as if whoever lived there had to have a piece he could reach out and thumb.* From *The Big Sleep* by Raymond Chandler.[17]

Modern rooms are soft and slouchy. Nowadays we lounge. Our domestic deportment has become Americanised, laid-back. There is display in depth of carpet pile, heaps of cushions, long wheel-base sofas as cushy as stretch limousines. These sofas are part of the little nuclear chair-family called the three piece suite. The three piece suite is an important item of display. Its comfy huddle is like a little encampment, the very centre of the home. It forms a miniature stadium for watching the world as shown on TV, the overstuffed chairs like a trio of fat people viewing a near-fatal accident.

The living room is a stage upon which prize objects are paraded. Every house is a show house. Its contents are icons, object lessons. In the case of the newly affluent they testify to a hard-earned passage. The plaster donkey from the Costa brays of travel as once did the exotic objects of returned colonials. Some living rooms are so taken up with cherished objects that they resemble the seventeenth century 'closets' of the *virtuosi*, men of learning and taste with a liking for 'cabinets of curiosities'.

> *The smaller room was something like a chapel in a cathedral or a grotto in a cave, for the booming sound of the traffic in the distance suggested the soft surge of waters, and the oval mirrors, with their silver surface, were like deep pools trembling beneath starlight. But the comparison to a religious temple of some kind was the more apt of the two, for the little room was crowned with relics.* From *Night and Day* by Virginia Woolf.[18]

But instead of stuffed armadillos we have plaster donkeys, instead of Chinese cups and Persian bowls we have mail order detritus. Their only merit is that they have been chosen, tended and cleaned. Cleaning is an act of appropriation. The ultra-clean modern object has a sort of super-real quality, as if it still belongs to the hypermarket from which it was bought, but it is the act that matters. The scouring of the doorstep of an old working-class terrace house was not only an announcement of a well-run home; it was like leaving a spore or scent and had an identical purpose, to demarcate territory.

As soon as their owner ceases to be, the objects he or she has chosen become 'contents', stuff for the beady eye of a house-clearer, as meaningless as the job-lot *bric-à-brac* of a pub or restaurant, for these are places that fake domesticity and the precious relationship between owner and owned. That is why we view such impedimentia with suspicion and the furnishings of a living room with respect, however low their intrinsic worth. Appropriation and care create their own value.

It is not only the newly-affluent who have a history problem. The upper-middle classes suffer the burden of the English country house, the interior design of which suffuses the repro heritage industry. Country house style is almost invariably pompous and vulgar, but here is the dream:

> *It was a deep, comfortable room with books lining the walls to the ceiling, the sort of room a man would move from never, did he live alone, solid chairs beside a great open fireplace, baskets for the two dogs in which I felt they never sat, for the hollows in the chairs had tell-tale marks. The long windows looked out upon the lawns, and beyond the lawns to the distant shimmer of the sea. There was an old quiet smell about the room, as though the air in it was little changed, for all the sweet lilac scent and the roses brought to it throughout the early summer. Whatever air came to this room whether from the garden or from the sea, would lose its first freshness, becoming part of the un-changing room itself, one with the books, musty and never read, one with the scrolled ceiling, the dark panelling, the heavy curtains.* From *Rebecca* by Daphne Du Maurier.[19]

The design firm of Colefax & Fowler recreated that look for an upper-middle class which had lost the ability to create it unselfconsciously as a by-product of a way of life. The rooms of John Fowler and his successors signal class superiority—all awful colours (the muds and greens of England), pictures of pricey animals, lumpen furniture, cluttered tablescapes, glazed chintzes, important curtains, a redundancy of upholstered pieces, oversized objects, overblown proportions and chandeliers (the decor equivalent of champagne). There is a small industry devoted entirely to maintaining the fiction of a style of pleasing dog-eared, dog-haired shabbiness.

Even apart from being full of erzatz heritage, the interior design magazines are not a pretty read. A branch of money porn, they are pin-up books of naked egos, those of the clever people who made such glittering assemblages of chattels to furnish their quarters. It seems that the rich no longer have

Class superiority by
Colefax & Fowler

rooms; they have *mises-en-scène*. A *mise-en-scène* is the environment of an event or an arrangement of stage properties. The evidence however suggests that the environment *is* the event.

In the *mise-en-scène* of a London fashion designer the hall is dark, *cinéma noir* dark you understand, not gloomy. There is an Indonesian Buddha by the shuttered window and the plants on the table look as if they've had something complicated done to them. Inside the room, a brace of Georgian wing chairs upholstered in cream shantung silk and bearing leopardskin cushions flank a Chinese spirit house placed on a full-skirted medium's table. In front of mirrored panels (reminding us of the time when mirrors were carried over the Alps on the backs of peasants) stands an eighteenth century Italian console and below it is a Japanese lacquered chest. There is another Buddha and then another. If they did anything but just squat the place would be crawling with them. The walls are painted lavender and some of it seems to have got into the parquet floor. The lavender follows you closely into the dining area where metallic chairs from Sheridan Oakley surround a table whose Paisley cloth is overlaid with a Guatemalan shawl whose bright colours

Standing jokes and a bid for the exquisite—a 'me' room, deadly precious

would look fine on a Guatemalan mountain peasant. Two gilded reindeer square up on a shelf, a chubby plaster lion roars back at some ferocious wallpaper, terracotta angels attempt flight and the distressed decorative columns are blanched by sensory overload. It is a spectacular piece of showing-off.

We learn that the occupant had a previous incarnation of this flat illustrated in an earlier issue. Maybe he's trying to get a message through from the other side (that is, whatever place you get to when you go over the top), a plea for help maybe.

Room egotism has many forms. Minimalism is another, boasting sheer space and an apparent austerity of mind. The incorporation of *objects trouvé* speaks of energy and quirky taste. The flat of a woman photographer includes a sink dug out of the back garden, taps made from plumbing pipes and a black living room (reminiscent of a surrealist tobacco advertisement). There are blazing nuts and bolts forming a fire-cum-sculpture. We are told that the woman photographer had the niche created because she felt the need for a primitive pyre in the house—'something with a religious feel'.

The living rooms of our very own *fin de siècle*, freed of much of the burden of correctness, are more than ever 'look at me' rooms, heavily edited autobiographies telling of taste, experience and knowledge; flattering self-portraits, their contents signalling the owner's image of himself to guests. They are referential assemblages, works of imagination, fictions, narratives, rooms which are their own view.

Scott Fitzgerald tells how Gatsby, the great consumer, simultaneously loses his ego and the alter-ego of his rooms:

> *He hadn't once ceased looking at Daisy, and I think he revalued everything in his house according to the measure of response it drew from her well-loved eyes. Sometimes too, he stared around at his possessions in a dazed way, as though in her actual and astounding presence none of it was any longer real. Once he nearly toppled down a flight of stairs.*[20]

It is easy to deduce the occupant from his billet, perhaps more of the occupant than he wishes to reveal, for no matter how they try people give themselves away.

> *The gentle-eyed, horse-faced maid let me into the long grey and white upstairs sitting-room with the ivory drapes tumbled extravagantly on the floor and the white carpet from wall to wall. A screen star's boudoir, a place of charm and seduction, artificial as a wooden leg.'* From *The Big Sleep* by Raymond Chandler.[21]

You know the kind of girl who will enter, and you don't need to be Philip Marlowe to solve the cases of the fashion designer and the photographer. The first demonstrates the eclecticism and frivolity of fashion, draining every object of its original significance. In the second, the suspect lives in a black-lined Kodak film box and her rooms are more photographs than reality. But these rooms go further than just being self-advertisements. Their makers are attempting to overwhelm the guest, even to control behaviour. This is room domination. It is nearly as old as houses.

The great house, in which the division of sensibilities into rooms was paralleled by nuances of conduct and the growth of ritual, provides a full kit for the sponsorship of behavioural transitions from room to room. The processional quality of dining in such a house demands fine calibrations of attitude and demeanour. Pre-dinner drawing room behaviour had to be

A photographer's 'womb room', black as
the inside of a Kodak box. Room as photograph
and nothing much besides

45 · HOME ENTERTAINMENT

adjusted in the dining room, which ensured that people knew their exact place by virtue of the long hierarchical table. (The round table arrived in more egalitarian times.)

The very clutter of some rooms and the extreme neatness of others inhibits movement and sets the behavioural agenda. Custom insists, rooms dictate; you can never really make yourself at home.

> *Pierre was shown into the little drawing-room, in which it was impossible to sit down without disturbing the symmetry, tidiness and order; and consequently it was quite comprehensible, and not strange, that Berg should magnanimously offer to disturb the symmetry of the armchair or of the sofa for an honoured guest, and apparently finding himself in miserable indecision in the matter, should leave his guest to solve the question of selection.* From *War and Peace* by Leo Tolstoy.[22]

Designer rooms only *seem* to be an abdication from the imposition of personality on home. The message they give is of pure, intimidating money:

> *... The meeting took place in what I called the 'processed leather room—it was one of six done for us by a decorator from Sloanes years ago, and the term stuck in my head. It was the most decorator's room, an angora wool carpet the colour of dawn, the most delicate gray imaginable—you could hardly walk on it; and the silver panelling and leather tables and creamy pictures and slim frailties looked so easy to stain that we could not breath hard in there, though it was wonderful to look into from the door when the windows were open and the curtains whispered querulously against the breeze.* From *The Last Tycoon* by Scott Fitzgerald.[23]

Room domination, a still from *Citizen Kane*

Full circle

These are extremes of room domination; rigorous rooms, totalitarian interior design, rooms which brook no dissent. The room, carrying the full weight of its author, is stronger than the guest.

Miss Marple understood then just what her friend had meant when she said the dead girl wasn't real.

And across the old bearskin hearthrug there was sprawled something new and crude and melodramatic: The flamboyant figure of a girl ... The face was heavily made-up, the powder standing out grotesquely on its blue swollen surface, the mascara of the lashes lying thickly on the distorted cheeks, the scarlet of the lips looking like a gash. The fingernails were enamelled in a deep blood-red and so were the toenails in their cheap silver sandal shoes. It was a cheap, tawdry, flamboyant figure—most incongruous in the solid old-fashioned comfort of Colonel Bantry's library. From *The Body in the Library* by Agatha Christie.[24]

That says a great deal about the English attitude to home. Here is the traditional, fundamental divide between upper-middle class shabbiness and working class flash baroque. The girl's decor just didn't match. It is as if someone had smuggled in a brassy MFI magazine rack. And here too is the nightmare of invasion. Invasion of the home is, as burglary victims will testify, the next worst thing to invasion of the person. It's a kind of room rape.

The party is a controlled invasion. We have exported most kinds of entertainment outside the home to places of specialised fun, not least to public houses. The party represents the greatest surrender of privacy. It can be simultaneously both the celebration and the abandonment of personality:

'Every time she gave a party she had this feeling of being something not herself, and that every one was unreal in one way; much more real in another.' From *Mrs Dalloway* by Virginia Woolf.[25]

Most modern rooms are inappropriately shaped and dressed for the party role. They represent domestic quarantine and lack public ease. Everybody can identify that rare thing 'a great room for a party'. The party is a complex piece of room ecology. Party room ecology demands focal points and also the capacity for flow. Behaviour will mimic the form it can inhabit. The first guests will stand by the fireplace, traditional symbol of welcome and a reliable anchor in the social turbulence of random meetings. Proximity to this icon gives confidence and control:

> *In the formal drawing-room of Stone Lodge, standing on the hearth-rug, warming himself before the fire, Mr Bounderby delivered some observations to Mrs Gradgrind on the circumstance on its being his birthday. He stood before the fire, partly because it was a cool spring afternoon, though the sun shone; partly because the shade of Stone Lodge was always haunted by the ghost of damp mortar; partly because he thus took up a commanding position, from which to subdue Mrs Gradgrind.* From *Hard Times* by Charles Dickens.[26]

Later party guests will establish themselves by other room-marks, perhaps a window or a table. When the room is full other guests will stand in doorways or at the bottom of staircases, that is to say, in bottlenecks on routes the better to facilitate chance encounters. Others will inhabit the kitchen because there is the smallest possible degree of formality in such a location. Interconnecting rooms and terraces to promenade on and through promote a feeling of freedom and ease (as did the *en suite* salons of Palladio). Galleries—the commanding heights—provide the opportunity to feel the spectator's superiority but when the party is over the room is abandoned and sad. Here is an inkling of another English preoccupation—the abandonment and decay of rooms, in novels this often is a metaphor for death.

> *And inside, as we wandered through the Marie Antoinette music-room and Restoration Salons, I felt that there were guests concealed behind every couch and table, under orders to be breathlessly silent until we had passed through . . .*
>
> *His house had never seemed so enormous to me as it did that night when we hunted through the great rooms for cigarettes. We pushed aside curtains that were like pavilions, and felt over innumerable feet of dark wall for electric light switches—once I tumbled with a sort of splash upon the keys of a ghostly piano. There was an inexplicable amount of dust everywhere, and the rooms were musty, as though they hadn't been aired for many days.* From *The Great Gatsby* by Scott Fitzgerald.[27]

> *A fire had been lately kindled in the damp old-fashioned grate, and it was more disposed to go out than to burn up, and the reluctant smoke which hung in the room seemed colder than the cleaner air—like our own marsh mist. Certain wintry branches of candles on the high chimney-piece faintly lighted the chamber; or, it would be more expressive to say, faintly troubled its darkness. It was spacious, and I dare say had once been handsome, but every discernible thing in it was covered with dust and mould, and dropping to pieces.* From *Great Expectations* by Charles Dickens.[28]

No display, no pride, no home; the creature has abandoned his quarters and the tracks he made in them fade. His rooms slip toward oblivion, as all rooms do, except in memory and museums.

The Geffrye Museum in East London consists of rooms strung out along a corridor, each furnished in the style of a period. You start in the seventeenth century and you end up outside the 1950s room staring fascinated but without comprehension at your childhood, the god of things as they were. It's like being a ghost.

Then you pass back down the corridor. Plasterwork gives way to wood, the rooms become plainer and darker and then they stop. In a perfected Geffrye museum there would be other, earlier rooms. A longer dark corridor, like those secret passages in detective stories which always end in surprising places, would pass centuries of Anglo-Saxon hall houses and then—at the very beginning of the corridor, deep in time, there would be light, elegance, warmth, civilisation, the shock of the ancient.

This British Atlantis was Roman Britain. Its villas were so advanced you could almost believe, like a fuddled fantast, that space travellers had been and gone. But no, the people who lived in these villas were mostly Romanised Britons. Their great country houses had hot air under-floor and wall heating, window-glass, elaborate bathing places including what we know as Swedish and Turkish baths, painted wall plaster, intricate mosaic floors, rooms with apses and rooms shaped as octagons, grand dining rooms and private chambers to taste.

The simplest and earliest type of villa was the cottage house consisting of a couple of rooms with a through passage. To this was added a front sun-trap verandah and large projecting rooms at each end built for the heads of the family. Thus we have the classic winged corridor house from about AD 100. The wings grew longer, eventually turning to enclose a courtyard with a gate-house. Does all this begin to sound familiar? It is, but the Romano-British were better housed than the Elizabethans more than a millenium later. It took even longer than that for Roman ideas to return more fully through the agency of Inigo Jones via Vitruvius and Palladio. But, strangely enough, the nearest popular approximation to the plan of the Romano-British villa can be seen in the bungalows of the 1920s.

Romano-British culture ceased around AD 367 and it would seem that the barbarian invaders seldom as much as squatted in the mansions they found. Nobody dwelt there any more. Everything was destroyed, but there is evidence enough remaining of great rooms. There was a villa in Gloucestershire which had a dining room whose domed roof was supported on four columns. Its floor was embellished with an Orphean mosaic, and there was a fountain.

There is another house in Gloucestershire, a new one, which is an under-

Mole Manor—ancient lights

 world dwelling in which Rat and Badger would have been comfortable. This Mole Manor was designed by the architect Arthur Quarmby. Its rooms (or curtained recesses) are arranged around a courtyard covered by a dome supported on four columns. In the courtyard there is a pool but it is not the turquoise tank of suburban display. It refers to something more ancient. From the outside the house appears as a grass mound, a tumulus. It is both turf, hut and mansion. Somehow it contains the spirit of the Romano-British villa, the openness of modernity and that aspect of the English attitude towards home which is to do with rurality, burrows and closeness to the earth. All our houses are haunted. Our rooms have long memories; they tell home lies, home truths.

A Greek kline of the fifth century BC, illustrated
on an Attic vase. Note the ionic capital-like
volutes which raise the head end of the kline
and support the bolster. The scene shows
Heracles being visited by Athena

CHAPTER TWO

PRIVATE PARTS

DAN CRUICKSHANK

THE AUTHOR WOULD LIKE TO THANK THE FOLLOWING FOR THEIR
HELP IN WRITING THIS CHAPTER: VIRGINIA BUSWELL,
DAVID TURNBULL, ANDREW SAINT, NICHOLAS COOPER,
NEIL BURTON, ANTHONY QUINEY, DENIS SEVERS AND
DOUGLAS BLAIR.

And so to bed . . .

The search for privacy in the home is associated with the development of two rooms—the bedroom and the bathroom. But there is more to this search than their story. The evolution of the furniture and fittings they contain—notably the bed itself—constitute a significant subplot, while the changing relationship of these rooms with the other rooms of the house adds yet another dimension to the story.

The story of the bed begins before the story of the bedroom, for the bedroom as we now know it—a private room intended primarily if not solely for sleeping—did not join the community of rooms until well into the eighteenth century.

Early references to beds are numerous. From the beginning beds were associated with pomp and power as well as with sensuality. Polycletus of Larissa records[1] that, in the third century BC, Alexander the Great would conduct business and hold court while reclining on a golden couch placed in the middle of his tent and surrounded by his bodyguard.

The Bible as much as the writings of the Greeks furnishes evidence for the association of beds and sensuality. One of the best of these references comes from the Book of Proverbs:

I have decked my bed with coverings of tapestry, with carved works, with fine linen from Egypt. I have perfumed my bed with myrrh, aloes and cinnamon, come, let us take our fill of love until the morning: let us solace ourselves with love, for the goodman is not at home, he is on a long journey.

Euripides makes clear the connection between beds and marriage. Alcestis, who has agreed to surrender her life in place of her husband, mildly upbraids her couch for its role in her downfall:

Dear bed, here I first gave myself to him; and now I die for him. Goodbye, my marriage bed! I do not hate you, but you have been my death, you alone, since I refused to fail in a wife's duty. And now another wife will possess my place here. She may be happier; more true she could not be![2]

Several questions are raised by these references. What exactly did these early beds look like, where were they located in the home, and was communal or solitary sleeping favoured? Tutankhamen's bed confirms that, as early as

Roman couch and bed cubicle of the first century AD from Pompeii. The richly frescoed walls and the decorated floor reveal that this was a room of some importance. The couch is made of ebony inlaid with ivory, paste and semi-precious stones

1350 BC, there were beds that look very much like the ones we know today—
that is, a functional design consisting of a sleeping surface raised above the
dirt of the floor and embellished with various appropriate decorations. In the
case of Tutankhamen's bed, the mattress frame, made of ebony and sheathed
with gold, is supported by carved timber lion legs.[3]

The appearance of Greek couches (klines) is well-documented through
ceramic illustrations. Klines combined the function of a bed for sleeping, a
couch for eating and a sofa for daytime repose. Made of wood and inlaid
with ornament of gold, silver, tortoise-shell or ivory, the general appearance
of the kline is now best known from imitations made during the classical

revival of the early nineteenth century. Typically, klines had a base made from leather cords supporting a mattress which was covered with wool blankets, fleece or skins. Sheets would have been a rarity. Pillows, or bolsters, were placed at both head and foot. Quite where the couch was placed within the Greek house it is hard to say, beyond that sleeping chambers (thalamos) were located off the central hall (megaron). But it seems that sleeping could be a communal affair, with several couches to a room—'our room had seven couches fine while another boasted nine' Phrynichus wrote in the fifth century BC.[4] Also, as Euripides implied in *Alcestis*, the Greek couch could accommodate more than one occupant when occasion demanded.

The Romans adopted and developed the Greek sleeping arrangements. They evolved a variety of beds suitable for different purposes or locations; there were single beds (lectuli), double beds (lecti geniales), and richly decorated ceremonial marriage beds (nuptiale). Juvenal wrote in the first century AD: 'The bed that holds a wife is never free from wrangling and mutual bickerings; no sleep is to be got there! It is there that she sets upon her husband, more savage than a tigress that has her cubs.'[5] The placing of the beds within the Roman house has been revealed in great detail through the excavations of the remains of Pompeii, Herculaneum and Ostia. The atrium (the first court reached after entry from the street) had a number of alcoves or cubiculae placed off it. These included the tablinum, set opposite the main entrance, and which was used as a reception room, a dining room and also a study and store room for family archives. In here were set couches that could be used socially during the day and as beds at night. But most beds were in cubicles off the atrium. These cubicles were generally simple rooms containing a marble or stone dais on which was placed a mattress or bed. Separated from the atrium by curtains and lit by small windows set high in the wall, they were the forerunner of the private bedroom, though, as they might well contain more than one bed, privacy was only relative.

In larger houses a second court—the peristyle—was placed beyond the atrium with which it was connected by passageways set each side of the tablinum. This court, with its cloister-like colonnade and central garden, represented the inner sanctum and was the portion of the house reserved for the family and dedicated to comfort and privacy. In houses with peristyles, the atrium became the public face of the house beyond which only family members, slaves and intimate friends penetrated. It was around the peristyle, rather than around the atrium, that the dining room, saloon and the best bedrooms were located. These bedrooms would contain not mere mattresses on platforms but true beds with turned legs, head- and foot-boards, often decorated, and silk sheets. Also off the peristyle would be located bath houses and lavatory cubicles which drained into the common sewers.

A good impression of the sleeping and bathing arrangements found in the largest of Roman town houses and country villas is given by Pliny the Younger in the first century AD. He had villas at Laurentum and in Tuscany.[6] The Laurentum villa (near Ostia, in Latium) contained a group of five or six bedrooms of different shapes, including a round one, grouped at the western end of the villa and enjoying sea views. They were separated by a large dining room and were flanked on one side by a colonnaded inner court and on the other by a gymnasium which overlooked the sea. Nearby, on one side of the inner court, was a group of slaves' rooms, suggesting that quick and efficient bedroom servicing was a high priority. These rooms could double if required as extra guest bedrooms, for they were, wrote Pliny, 'quite presentable enough to receive guests'. Facing the slave rooms across the inner court was a group of bathrooms. In addition, there was Pliny's own suite of rooms with a master bedroom. This comprised a separate wing. In his Tuscan villa (near Tifernum), Pliny had a bedroom facing a dining seat and fountain which was:

> built of shining white marble, extended by folding doors which open straight out among the trees; its upper and lower windows all look out into the greenery above and below. A small alcove which is part of the room but separated from it contains a bed, and although it has windows in all its walls, the light inside is dimmed by the dense shade of a flourishing vine ... There you can lie and imagine you are in a wood, but without the risk of rain.

The well-developed sense of privacy as well as the subtle distinctions between different inhabitants and uses within the same house disappeared in Europe when Rome collapsed. By the eighth century AD, very different types of house and domestic habits had emerged. Now the house is dominated by a great hall and life is lived communally. The poem 'Beowulf' written in Old English in the eighth century but apparently recalling an earlier Scandinavian society throws light on the appearance of the early hall house and the way that life was lived in it. The hall was 'tall-gabled', had a high seat—that is, a dais at one 'end—benches, some of them 'figured and gold-worked' and was floored with timber. The inside walls were decorated with antlers, probably put to good use as night hooks for clothes and arms. At times of feasts 'gold-embroidered tapestries glowed' from the walls.

After feasting 'when evening came (the king) departed to his private bower ... to his couch' while the rest 'cleared away the benches, and covered the floor with beds and bolsters' so that 'the best at the feast bent to his hall-rest.' The grander members of the company seem to have slept on the dais for the hero of the poem 'Beowulf' 'mounts' to his bed. Clearing away the benches seems to have involved suspending some of them from the walls or roof timbers along with 'ring-stitched mail coats, mighty helmets ... spears ... and swords (in) racks'.[7] From the ancient and long-lived tradition of finding a place (or stead) in the hall for a bed comes our terms to 'make a bed' and bedstead.

By the eleventh century, the family in noble or wealthy households had followed the example of the king and taken themselves off to private sleeping quarters, leaving the hall to the lower orders. This habit had percolated through to the merchant and yeoman classes by the late thirteenth century, by which time a very particular type of house had evolved which closely reflected the needs and aspirations of the society that built it. These houses were still organised around a central double-height hall but were far more rational and compact in plan and designed for maximum convenience. The most sophisticated of this type of timber-framed hall houses built for the newly emergent middle classes is now known as the Wealden. And if this makes it sound like a modern house-builders' type, this is not far off the

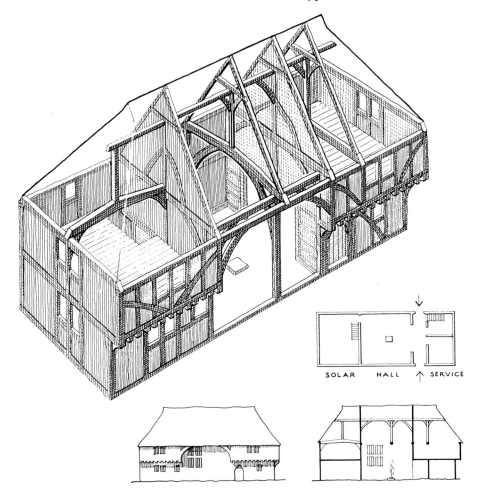

SOLAR   HALL   ↑ SERVICE

Illustrations of a fifteenth century Wealden house by Richard Harris. In the centre is the hall, rising the full height of the house. On the left are the family quarters, and on the right is the service wing

The first floor front bedroom at 58 French Street has been restored to the appearance it may have had in 1300. It contains two box beds, each capable of sleeping two, and which are given privacy by means of ample bed curtains

mark. The Wealden hall house was produced in thousands from the late fourteenth to the early sixteenth centuries in the south-east of England, particularly in the Weald of Kent and in East Anglia.

The form of this house is worth a detailed look, for it tells us much about the attitudes of the medieval middle class to privacy and to convenience. The central double-height hall, open to the handsome, well-wrought roof construction, was the public and formal focus of the house. Here the yeoman would hold court like a little king, sitting at a high table with his dependents, guests and retainers seated according to rank and status either with him or on benches below. All were heated by a fire burning on a hearth placed in the centre of the hall. The dignity of the scene would have been little compromised by the fact that the central hearth was also used for cooking

so that the hall filled with the smell of food as well as with smoke. Facing the high table was a screens passage. Beyond the screen were (at ground level) the buttery, the pantry, a food preparation area and possibly a dairy and a bakehouse. Above these offices, and reached via a very modest stair, would be guest lodgings. These might also incorporate a garderobe in the form of a shoot taking sewage into a ditch or cesspit. A second set of chambers on two storeys behind the high table allowed the family to relax and sleep leaving the hall to the nocturnal pastimes of the servants.[8]

Number 58 French Street in Southampton is a fascinating permutation of the type which, thanks to a recently-completed archaeological investigation

58 French Street, Southampton, a recently repaired merchant's house of *c.* 1300. The private family bedroom was above the shop, with great hall and kitchen wing behind

and restoration by English Heritage, throws new light on the way in which people lived in these modest urban hall houses. The building was constructed about 1300 to serve as a shop with dwelling-place for a merchant trading with Bordeaux. It is essentially a rural hall house swung round 90 degrees so that the main entry is through the short flank elevation rather than directly into the hall. In this way a free-standing type could be adapted to serve on a restricted urban site as a terrace house. The hall (behind the shop) possessed a high table, but heating was not by means of an open central hearth but from a fireplace with a stack and firehood. Beyond the hall is the office, which also has a fireplace and a masonry stack. If these fireplaces are contemporary with the original construction of the house (as is perfectly possible) then they provide an extremely early example of the move away from the open hearth.

Above the shop and the office are chambers connected by a gallery that runs above a screens passage set along one side of the hall. The chamber above the shop, which has a view onto the street, seems to have been the room in which the family slept and relaxed in private during the day. Perhaps they shivered for neither of the upper chambers contains a fireplace. However, evidence suggests that there were at least two beds in the room and each bed could have slept two, so the chamber made a far-from-private bedroom. Clearly, bed curtains in rooms such as this served more than just a decorative function.

Geoffrey Chaucer, in the Reeve's narration from *The Canterbury Tales*, which was written in the late fourteenth century, suggests not only that communal sleeping was usual in the yeoman class, but also explains why, and hints at the arrangement of a family bedroom. The Miller in the story:

> *in his chamber made a bed*
> *with clean white sheets and blanket fairly spread,*
> *Ten foot from his, upon a sort of shelf,*
> *His daughter had a bed all by herself.*
> *Quite close in the same room, they were to lie*
> *All side by side, no help for it, and why?*
> *Because there was no other in the house.*[9]

Beds in the fourteenth century were flimsy almost temporary affairs that were easy to move around the house or to transport from one building to another; their greatest ornament was their hangings, which could all-but conceal the rudimentary joinery of the box-like construction. These hangings, giving privacy and protection from draughts, were used only on the better sort of beds. Junior members of the family or favoured servants who had graduated from mattresses on the floor, would have slept in truckle, trundle, or trussed beds—that is, low beds on wheels which slid under the main one when not in use or folding beds that were concealed during the day when the family bedchamber was used as a parlour. Other furniture in these early bedchambers included hutches or chests, and perches (or rods) for the storage or hanging of garments and bedding.

While the modest hall house of the fourteenth century was a milestone in the achievement of privacy for the yeoman class, it was in larger houses of the same period that new ideas concerning convenience and privacy were pioneered. These houses—usually the product of gradual expansion and organic in character—were generally arranged around one or more courts and could be more or less fortified. But what they all possessed was a range containing a great hall and beside it a great chamber or parlour. Haddon Hall in Derbyshire furnishes an excellent example. It was began in the late twelfth century and acquired its existing great hall and parlour *c.*1370. Other ranges contained kitchen (often as at Haddon Hall set on the same axis as the hall), chapel, stables and chambers of various sizes. By the middle of the fourteenth century a noble family living in a large courtyard house had removed itself almost entirely from the noise and dirt of the great hall to a more private and dignified—though no less formal—life in the great chamber and parlour.

The change was dramatic and it was seen by poor people as a betrayal. The removal of the lord from the hall meant an end to its indiscriminate hospitality. As William Langland lamented in his *Vision of Piers Ploughman* written *c.*1375:

> *When the lord and lady eat elsewhere every day of the week, their hall is a sorry, deserted place. And the rich nowadays have a habit of eating by themselves in private parlours—for the sake of the poor, I suppose—or in a special chamber with a fireplace of its own. So they abandon the main hall, which was made for men to eat their meals in—and all this in order to save money.*[10]

The family not only dined regularly in the great chamber (only eating in the great hall on festivals and state occasions) but entertained itself and its guests here. Members of the family or honoured guests may also have slept there, for the great chamber was the best room in the fourteenth century house, and the best room in the house often contained the best bed in the house. It seems that a great bed surmounted by a canopy possessed much of the symbolic value of a canopy-crowned throne; both added to the grandeur of a room and conferred dignity on the proceedings that took place around or on it. But it seems unlikely that such a bed would have been in regular use while the great chamber remained in communal use, for one of the characteristics of the fourteenth century revolution in domestic habits was the growth in popularity among the nobility for a more private bedchamber and for 'lodgings', that is, for suites of interconnected rooms forming a self-contained apartment.

The appearance of one of these new bedchambers, and of the way in which it was used, is described in the mid-fourteenth century story of 'Sir Gawain and the Green Knight'. It is clear immediately that a great advance in comfort and convenience was provided and that the use was something of the order of a bedsitting room. Sir Gawain, a guest at the castle of the Green Knight, is led to:

> ... *a beautiful room where the bedding was noble.*
> *The bed-curtains, of brilliant silk with bright gold hems,*
> *Had skillfully-sewn coverlets with comely panels,*
> *And the fairest fur on the fringes was worked.*
> *With ruddy gold rings on the cords ran the curtains;*
> *Tapestry of Toulouse silk and Turkestan stuff*
> *Furbished the walls and the floor underfoot as well.*[11]

Sir Gawain then sat on a chair 'gorgeously decked with cushions on quilted work' beside a 'chimneyed hearth where charcoal burned' and in front of him a trestle table was erected and 'covered with a cloth shining clean and white, and set with silver spoon, salt cellar and napkin'. Sir Gawain washed and then 'went to his meat'—several soups and 'fish of all kinds'.

Upstairs, downstairs
and in milady's chamber

The close relationship in the late Middle Ages between great chambers, beds and dining is confirmed by a mid fifteenth century manuscript entitled *Order of service* and written for those waiting upon the higher nobility.[12] This states that the bed of the lord of the house was in the great chamber and reveals that putting the lord and his wife to bed required the attention of nine servants who processed into the great chamber carrying such night-time necessities as a silver jug of beer, two large pots of wine and two kinds of bread. The bread and wine were tasted by the yeoman of the chamber. Each item that the noble pair might use was treated with a reverential deference akin to church ceremonies and was kissed before being put in place. Finally, all items were covered or wrapped in napkins to protect them from the birds that flitted freely into and around the lofty chamber.

In the morning, a yeoman servant brought clothes folded in a sheet to the outer chamber or anteroom. Gentlemen ushers then took those garments in and dressed the lord. Presumably, gentlewomen provided the same service for the lady. Use would be made of the garderobe located off the great chamber. Washing was by means of a basin and ewer. Baths were fairly complex affairs involving the erection of screens in front of the fire and much douching with water and manhandling of heavy timber tubs. The quick morning dip seems to be a thing for the future, even in noble households. After such ablutions, the lord attended seven o'clock Mass in his closet—an intimate, cosy and convenient private room. The closet, a small richly decorated and furnished chamber, had obviously already achieved its character as a room for the most private and personal of pursuits.

While the lord and his lady are at Mass, the servants strip off the bed linen and set up a trestle supporting a 'breakfast board' at the bed's end. Thirteen servants, including gentlemen cupbearers, carvers and servers, could be involved in the breakfast ceremony. Again, everything was tasted and everything that the nobles were to use personally was kissed before being laid out—except for the spoon and knife (the fork had yet to be invented). A noble visitor would breakfast with the lord in the great chamber but at a separate 'long board'. When the nobles had finished, the gentlemen servants broke their own fast in an outer chamber, leaving the great hall to the yeoman servants who ate there along with other lower servants. After 1500 the habits of the upper classes quickly filtered through to a lower social level. There was a general migration of middling families from the great hall to the great chamber, a move that had profound architectural consequence—not least of which was the great hall's decline into servants' hall and then by 1600, to becoming a mere entrance vestibule.

The Old Hall, a manor house built in Radnorshire in the 1570s, reveals these architectural consequences as well as telling us much about late sixteenth century ideas about privacy and convenience. It was during this century that privacy came to be valued for its own sake. It was seen by an increasingly sophisticated and educated aristocracy as well as by well-to-do merchants as a mark of distinction, in opposition to the vulgar love of open display indulged in by previous generations.

Ground and first floor plans of the Old Hall, showing the great hall, the great chamber and the panelled bed-chamber

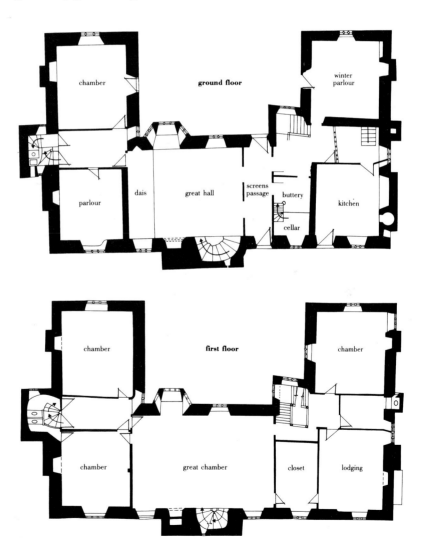

(ABOVE) Detail of the garden front of the Old
Hall, Radnorshire, built *c.* 1570. The open door
reveals a view along the screens passage. The
timber gable stands above the ornate staircase
which was added in 1638. (OPPOSITE TOP) Detail
of the first floor great chamber. The door to
the left of the fireplace leads to a stone spiral
staircase which descends to the great hall

(RIGHT) The first floor bedchamber in the family wing of the Old Hall. This room lies behind the 'dais' end of the great chamber and is one of the most important of the private family rooms

Separate rooms were required for the display of objects, or just for reading—a pastime that became increasingly popular as literacy increased and books became cheaper and more readily available. These new aspirations demanded architectural expression—notably a plan which allowed greater personal privacy, improved services providing more convenience and comfort and an increase in the number of rooms dedicated to specific, new uses. Study, gallery and bedchamber were among these. Many of these aspirations found expression at the Old Hall.

The form of the house is not pioneering, indeed it is a somewhat old fashioned E-plan type. The centre block still contains a great hall entered through a screens passage running between the front and back doors. The decline in the importance of the great hall is immediately apparent because, instead of rising sublimely into the roof timbers, it has been floored across to create another room above. This upper room is the great chamber. Both these rooms are provided with large fireplaces—a key element in the decline of the hall—because, as stacks and fireplaces became more common after 1500, the hall no longer needed to be open to the roof timbers to allow smoke to disperse from a central hearth. The planning possibilities offered by the general application of new fireplace technology coupled with the decline in the importance of the hall was quickly realised. Usurping the upper volume of the hall made possible the provision in even a relatively modest and compact house of a great chamber. So even modest families were able to indulge in the fashion for leaving the hall to the servants and moving into an upper-level great chamber where, with satisfactory symbolism, they could dine above their inferiors messing in the great hall below.

The combination of the family dining in state in the great chamber with the elevation of this chamber to the first floor meant that staircases suddenly became very important. No longer were they just a means of moving around a house but key elements in the progress from entrance door to the main family room on the first floor and for the procession of dishes from ground floor kitchen to family dining table. The Old Hall possessed three staircases in 1570, none of which lived up to its new importance. The kitchen was still in the traditional position in a wing beyond the screens passage. This wing contained one of the house's three stone spiral staircases; possibly food was carried by this route from the kitchen to the great chamber. But a more likely progression was by way of the formal stair set beside the fireplace in the great hall and which rises directly to the great chamber.

The kitchen wing is balanced by a family wing set, as was traditional, behind the dais end of the great hall. This was the private side of the house accessible only to family, friends and of course to the ubiquitous servants. Its rooms, connected by a family staircase, would have been used as parlours and bedchambers—the best of which seems to have been on the first floor directly beyond the high-table end of the great chamber for this main room is provided with its own garderobe, a small room reached through a narrow passage and provided with a shoot into a pit at the foot of the wall. This grand and convenient bedroom probably contained the best bed in the house, although it is possible that this exalted piece of furniture continued to hold state in the great chamber, where it would occasionally have given dignified rest to favoured guests.

Usually guests would have slept in the lodgings above the kitchen; a set of rooms provided with their own spacious garderobe discharging into a large cesspit and with separate access from the exterior by the staircase set beside the kitchen. The three staircases in the Old Hall, and their related landings, make a great contribution to the smooth working of the house. They mean that it is never necessary to reach one room by walking through another, as was often the case in rambling medieval houses, and all rise up to the second floor where servants, children and inferior visitors would have found beds below the roof timbers.

Sleeping arrangements in the Old Hall's humble contemporary, the rural cottage, is recorded by Rowland Parker in his study of the village of Foxton in Cambridgeshire. An examination of wills revealed that:

> no household . . . was without a bed of some sort, and that the bed takes pride of place amongst the owner's possessions. We are frequently told in detail what was on the bed . . . and sometimes exactly where it stood. 'A bed with all things perteyninge thereto, as mattris, fetherbed, shete, Bollster, pillowe, a blanket and a coverlet with a Bedstead standinge in the parler by the street.'[13]

Most sixteenth century Foxton cottages were single-storey and consisted only of a hall and parlour. It was not until the 1620s that beds were placed upstairs 'in the chamber', standing on a floor that may well have been inserted into the upper part of the hall of a fifteenth or sixteenth century house.

The Old Hall has one last story to tell, and this has to do with one of the great moments in British architecture—the arrival of the prodigious timber staircase. In 1638 the humble stone spiral stair beside the kitchen was removed (along with the adjoining porch and porch room) to allow for the installation of a piece of virtuoso joinery which at last provided a satisfactory route for the progress of food from the kitchen to the high table in the great chamber. This staircase reflects a late sixteenth century penchant for large-scale and showy timber work, a passion that was perhaps expressed nowhere better than in the design and construction of beds. At the time the Old Hall was being built in the 1570s, England was at the dawn of the golden age of bed design. Previously, the hangings were the important element (as with the

The Great Bed of Ware measures 10 feet 8 ½ inches across, and illustrates the tremendous status that beds began to enjoy in the late sixteenth century when it was constructed

bed types recreated in 58 French Street, Southampton) but now massive and exotically carved joinery became the dominant feature.

From the late sixteenth century the bed began to enjoy an extraordinary status; it was not only richly decorated but could be of tremendous size, more a piece of architecture than a piece of furniture. The best example of this must surely be the Great Bed of Ware. It was made in the late sixteenth century, perhaps for an individual with an extraordinary sense of self-importance (the bed measures 10 feet $8\frac{1}{2}$ inches across), but more probably for the landlord of an inn with a good nose for publicity. If the latter were indeed the case, then the ploy was highly successful for as early as 1600 Shakespeare used the bed of Ware in *Twelfth Night* as a byword for gigantism.

The Great Bed of Ware is not typical in its origin or its size but it does provide an accurate insight into the priorities of its age; in the sixteenth and seventeenth centuries beds were large, elaborate, and richly decorated because they were among the more important of status symbols—they were the luxury fast cars of their age. As we have seen at Foxton, they usually received pride of place in wills. The fact that Shakespeare left his second-best bed to his wife has always been seen as a subtle slight on that unfortunate woman.

Indeed, the sixteenth and seventeenth century gentlemen was so proud of his bed that he put it to an amazingly wide range of uses.

In France, which became the centre of the cult of the bed, a man's dignity could be measured by the size and number of his beds. Here, in the early seventeenth century, the King attended Parliament in bed—his Lit de Justice—which was placed on a dais under a curtained canopy. Cardinal de Richelieu even took to the road in a bed-chariot when ill. François Premier was not the only king of France to invite a favoured friend, retainer or reconciled opponent to share his bed as a demonstration of esteem and symbol of political union.

The use of the bed as a tool of government and diplomacy gave rise to the term state bed, one that was more a symbol of power and prestige than for everyday (or night) use. This type of bed, and the ritual that surrounded it, had a profound influence on ideas of privacy and the organisation of rooms of the house. In England these ideas began to make their mark in the early seventeenth century. Before looking in detail at the state bed and the house plan it generated, we must examine the ideas that were established in Britain before the adoption of this French-inspired phenomenon.

The Old Hall, built during the 1570s represented a certain advance in privacy but was, as we have seen, still essentially late medieval in plan and little removed from the hall house prototype. But the last decades of the sixteenth century saw, through the architecture patronised by the court and aristocracy, the introduction of new ideas on house design and construction that were to transform life in the country house. These new ideas were in part a some- what belated response to the architectural revolution of the Italian Renaissance.

In late Tudor England architects such as Robert Smythson and John Thorpe displayed (in their house plans if not in their actual elevations) a familiarity with the works of sixteenth century Renaissance architects such as Sebastiano Serlio, and Andrea Palladio. These fresh foreign ideas fused with native design traditions and, coupled with the growing concern for domestic comfort, led to a startlingly new English architecture.

Hardwick Hall in Derbyshire was designed by Smythson in close col- laboration with his client, the Countess of Shrewsbury. It was built during the 1590s and embodies many new ideas. It was still provided with a great hall but turned round 90 degrees so that it is entered on its short side; this arrangement, and the symmetrical location of the hall in the centre of the house (stretching from back to front), relates more closely to the cubical halls found in Renaissance villas than to the great halls of English tradition. But, despite this change of character, the hall was still fitted with benches and long tables and the kitchen adjoined it in traditional manner.

The hall is double height, penetrating the first floor which is the level given over to family use with the low great chamber being used not only as the dining room but also as the main family living room. Above on the second floor are the state rooms, including the high great chamber, best bedchamber and long gallery. The prime apartments were placed on this level for the simple reason that the Countess was indulging in the then newly fashionable idea that the prospect offered from a room could be its greatest asset, an aim achieved in spectacular fashion by providing both first and second floor rooms with windows of huge size.

Privacy and direct access to bedchambers on both first and second floors was achieved by the use of a large number of staircases, extensive landings and passages placed as convenience demanded. This functional rather than formal approach may have led to greater comfort but did not produce a particularly elegant plan; indeed, the remarkable symmetry of the facade is contradicted by the interior with towering windows occasionally lighting small rooms or even being blocked internally by chimney stacks.

Although a house like Hardwick was clearly planned to combine convenience with display, it would be a mistake to assume that the age of complete personal privacy had finally arrived. For one thing, the running of a large early seventeenth century house depended on vast numbers of servants. As long as these servants had the run of the house, complete privacy was impossible. Attitudes had not yet hardened against the long-established tradition of communal living. Throughout the century people continued to live in bedrooms and often sleep in living rooms. It was still accepted that there could be more than one bed to a bedroom and that bed-sharing was not the exclusive activity of married couples or children. This long-lived habit of placing more than one bed in a room must explain the continuing popularity of the four-poster with its heavy hangings that kept out not only draughts but also prying eyes.

Samuel Pepys made frequent references in the latter half of the seventeenth century to the fact that 'the wench' (the maid) slept in the same room as he and his wife:

> ... *after we were all abed the wench (which lies in our chamber) caused us to listen of a sudden, which put my wife into such a fright that she shook every joint of her ... the wench went down and got a candle lighted ... and locking the door fast, we slept well but with a great deal of fear.*[14]

The description makes clear one reason why servants slept in the same chamber—to act as a kind of watchdog. They could be easily summoned when needed. The location of the servant within the bedroom is hinted at in another entry in Pepys' diary 'My wife and I in the high bed in our chamber, and Willet [the maid] in the trundle bed, which she desired to lie in by us'.[15]

Dalliance, drama and dignity

It is hard to say if, by the end of the seventeenth century, the bedroom had truly emerged as a distinct and private room used only for sleep and other night-time activities. The answer is probably, no. Not only did different classes live very different lives—there was little chance of privacy for the poor or for the servants of the better-off, but life for the rich was being confused by two conflicting aspirations. On the one hand there was the ever-growing demand for personal privacy. On the other, the growing fashion for the public display of the private parts of the house. This fashion demanded that the main rooms of the house be interconnected with all doors aligned to create a striking vista (or enfilade) through the house and to present an opportunity for a grand parade from room to room—a parade that culminated in the main bedroom with its state bed and adjoining closet or cabinet.

This was a fashion that came to England from Renaissance Italy (for example the Palazzo Medici in Florence of 1450), via France and in particular the court of Louis XIV, but the conflict between display and convenience had been noted and neatly summed up as early as the 1620s by Sir Henry Wotton, who was both a diplomat and a writer on architecture:

> *They so cast their partitions as when All doors are open, a man may see through the whole House; which doth necessarily put an intolerable servitude upon all the Chambers, save the Inmost, where non can arrive, but through the rest (an arrangement) grounded upon the fond ambition to display to a Stranger all our Furniture at one sight.*[16]

The enfilade plan reshuffled the state rooms to create not just a grand architectural vista through the house but also a route which could be used as a means of publicly conferring or withholding privilege. The system worked in a very simple manner. At a formal gathering, the depth of penetration along the axis of honour from saloon to antechamber, to withdrawing chamber, to bedchamber and closet indicated the status of the guest in the eyes of the host. The chambers got progressively richer and more exclusive in their nature the nearer they approached to the inner sanctum of the bedchamber, with its state bed and adjoining closet. At Chatsworth in Derbyshire, rebuilt for the Duke of Devonshire from the late 1680s to the design of William Talman and others, each room is decorated in a manner appropriate to its position and purpose on the axis of honour; an approach given a more particular focus at Chatsworth for the exalted position of the duke meant that these rooms could be conceived and decorated as a gathering place for the most exalted persons in the land. And, since the decorative scheme was executed in the 1690s, this meant King William III, Queen Mary and their court.

The great chamber on the second floor (now known as the state dining room) was the starting point of the route through the state apartments. It has a ceiling painted by Verrio on the theme of the virtues and vices showing the conflict between good and evil—a good subject for all in power to ponder upon. The anteroom (now called the state drawing room) has a ceiling painted by Laguerre showing the assembly of gods on Mount Olympus; again a good choice of subject because it was here that the court would have gathered while waiting to enter the presence chamber or to dine in the great chamber.[17] The next chamber in the sequence, the withdrawing or presence chamber (now the state music room) has a painted ceiling depicting Apollo being petitioned by his son Phaeton. It is in this room that the king would have sat in state to receive petitions. The bedchamber has a ceiling showing the triumph of Venus, while the ceiling of the closet shows Mercury being dispatched with the apple of the tree of knowledge—again an appropriate symbolism given the closet's function as an intimate meeting room for the king and his ministers in which matters of state could be discussed and from where, in theory, wise decisions would emanate.

Though a useful method for grading one's friends and other visitors, the fashion for the enfiladed state apartment was an unmitigated disaster from the point of view of privacy. Bedchambers not only continued to be placed beside or between rooms which were in noisy public use, but the enfilade system continued (and perhaps even revived) the old practice of placing beds in rooms that were not exclusively bedrooms. This meant that people continued to find themselves sleeping somewhere which turned out to be a through route from one room to another. And, of course, one of the most important chambers on the axis of honour was that which contained the state bed itself and this was very far from being a private room. Felbrigg Hall in Norfolk illustrates neatly the conflict between convenience and the fashion for enfiladed rooms. It was built around 1620 and was then only one room deep with virtually half of the ground floor given over to a great hall. In 1675 a wing was added behind the great hall to give the house an L-shaped plan. This wing, designed by William Samwell and not completed until the 1680s, was highly fashionable both externally and internally. It was given a brick garden elevation designed in the manner of Wren's contemporary

The state bedchamber in Powis Castle, Wales, was created *c.* 1665. It is in the taste of the seventeenth century court, with the bed placed in an alcove and separated from the rest of the chamber by a balustrade

metropolitan architecture. Inside it had, at ground level, a range of state rooms terminating in a cabinet and, at first floor, a row of bedchambers. At either levels the rooms could only be approached by passing one through another.

Interconnecting rooms may have suited the most formal patterns of late seventeenth-century life but certainly did not suit the more private existence which may have been attempted on the first floor at Felbrigg. If Felbrigg did orginally contain a state bedchamber on this floor (which would have made a little more sense of the floor plan), it is long gone. Existing beds date from the early nineteenth century when the rooms were redecorated.

The only fully accoutred seventeenth century state bedroom to survive in Britain is at Powis Castle in Wales. It was created about 1665 and retains its four-poster bed set in an alcove and behind an altar rail-like balustrade that separates the bed from the rest of the room. This room was the penultimate target on the enfilade processional route. The ultimate target was the bed itself. Or rather, to be invited within the balustrade and perhaps even into the closet beyond. This was the greatest compliment and mark of esteem and intimacy that the master of the house could bestow. If a king were inhabiting the state bedchamber then only favoured courtiers, privy councillors, cousins and brothers were permitted to cross the balustrade. Others, who were permitted to progress into the bedchamber but not beyond, stood outside the balustrade, looking at the king and his favourites much as a congregation watches Mass being celebrated in the chancel of the church with only those initiated or in a state of grace being permitted to participate. Louis XIV actually slept in his state beds—an act calculated to imbue him with the prestige of a man whose natural place of abode is the altar. Putting a state bed to practical use was actually most unusual and Louis seems to have been one of the only kings to do so. Charles II, whose English court was in many ways a pale imitation of that of Louis, used his state bedrooms not for sleeping in but as principal reception rooms and as rooms in which to take supper occasionally. In the adjoining cabinet or closet he held meetings with his ministers. These small and private rooms could usually be reached discreetly by a backstairs thus originating the term backstairs intrigue.

Even if the construction of a complete set of enfiladed state rooms was not possible, leading members of the court created state bedrooms in readiness for a possible royal visitor. The one at Powis Castle was constructed for Charles II, who failed to turn up. By this period any family with pretensions to grandeur had at least a state bed in their house, though not necessarily complete with balustrade, to indicate that they were a family of consequence and that royalty was liable to drop in for the night.[18]

In the royal usage of the state bedchamber lie the origins of the custom of the levée, an informal, though not always so, morning gathering when the grand could relax and be as it were a trifle off parade. Although levées could be held in more than one of the rooms of parade, it was the bedroom or dressing room that was principally favoured. Here both women and men received guests as they lay in or rose from their beds and while they were at their toilet. John Evelyn was delighted (and a little shocked) when he accompanied Charles II to the levée of the king's mistress in October 1683:

Following his majesty thro' into the Duchesse of Portsmouth's dressing roome within her bed-chamber, where she was in her morning loose garment, her maids combing her newly out of her bed, his majesty and the gallants standing about her.[19]

Lord Chesterfield, remembering life in the early eighteenth century, offered an account of the way in which the levée system was used and abused. His target is the Duke of Newcastle:

He generally made people of business wait two or three hours in the ante chamber while he trifled away that time with more insignificant favorites in his closet. When at last he came into his levée-room, he accosted, hugged, embraced and promised everybody, with seeming cordiality (and) with a degrading familiarity.[20]

Ironically enough, Chesterfield himself was not above such courtly discourtesy. The manipulation of the antechamber and the private backstairs contributed to his famous break with Dr Johnson, who had been kept waiting too long in an antechamber while Chesterfield chatted with Colley Cibber who had ascended to the Earl by a backstair. James Boswell explained 'When the door opened, and out walked Cibber, Johnson was so violantly provoked when he found for whom he had been so long excluded, that he went away in a passion, and never would return'.[21]

The fashion for the levée survived into the middle of the eighteenth century by which time even women of modest pretensions would receive guests from their beds or while away their mornings dressing with company present. William Hogarth in his 'Marriage à la Mode' series, painted in the early 1740s, suggests the hopelessly unfashionable ways of the poor little upstart countess by showing her revelling in the passé delights of the levée, attended by vulgar guests and held in a bedchamber containing a ponderous state bed still placed in an alcove in the seventeenth century French fashion.

Although 'the file of rooms' was seen in the late seventeenth century as 'the prime beauty' of the house,[22] there were significant (and in some cases very successful) attempts to find ways of reconciling the parade of interconnecting rooms with the demand for improved privacy. The corridor became one of the key components of this reconciliation and, strange as it

Plan of the main floor at Blenheim Palace, Oxfordshire, built in 1705–16 to the designs of Sir John Vanbrugh

 state

private

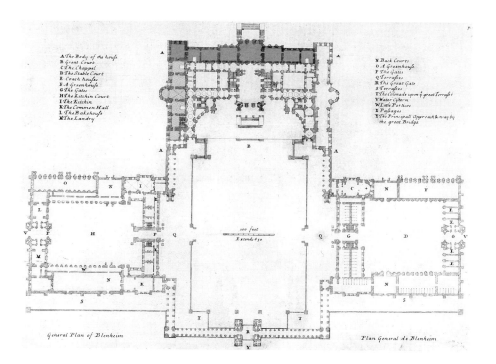

may seem, this familiar feature seems to have been regarded in the very early eighteenth century as something of a novelty. Certainly as late as 1716 Sir John Vanbrugh had to explain to his client for Blenheim Palace, the Duchess of Marlborough, what a corridor was: 'The corridore Madame is foreign, and signifies in plain English, no more than a passage'.[23]

As Vanbrugh implied, passages had been loitering around making themselves useful in country houses for generations so it is perhaps difficult to see what was so revolutionary about the corridor. Indeed, at Hengrave Hall in Suffolk (a courtyard house of the 1520s) a passage runs around three sides of the central court ensuring that main chambers are not used as through-routes. Similarly, passages are to be found at Hardwick Hall and became a feature of the double-pile house of the mid seventeenth century. Of this type Coleshill in Berkshire, built around 1650 to the design of Roger Pratt but burnt down in 1952, was an early and excellent example. Two parallel ranges of rooms were separated and served by corridors running the full length of the house and terminating in service stairs. This plan allowed for a high degree of privacy as main rooms were no longer on a through-route and bedchambers and closets could be gathered as self-contained apartments at the house corners. We shall see this develop further in the early eighteenth century.

Corridors, unlike passages, were more than mere routes of convenience. As Vanbrugh's work at Blenheim Palace (Oxfordshire) between 1705 and 1716 and at Castle Howard (North Yorkshire) between 1700 and 1726 reveals, corridors could be both functional and ornamental additions to the state apartments. At both houses Vanbrugh ran corridors parallel with the enfilade of state rooms. But these were not the modest passages found at Coleshill. They did make it possible to reach bedchambers without passing through drawing rooms and to remove night soil from closets and dressing rooms with maximum privacy. But they also played a major role in the architectural theatre of the interior by offering dramatic vistas and a new route of parade.

Corridors were deemed to be such a good idea and such a satisfactory way of improving the convenience of an interior that they were regularly added to existing country houses over the following hundred years. Notable examples are Longleat in Wiltshire which was built between 1554 and 1570 (perhaps by Smythson) and which was changed around 1805 when corridors were built within the house's inner courts and Wilton in Wiltshire, another courtyard house that dates mainly from the sixteenth and seventeenth centuries. A corridor block was constructed within its court in 1811 to a James Wyatt design. This meant that the splendid state rooms of Inigo Jones and John Webb, completed in 1649 and a pioneering example of the French enfilade taste, could be entered independently from the corridor and not by passing through one to reach the other.

The corridor at Blenheim. Running parallel to the state rooms, the corridor was an innovation which provided both a handsome additional route of parade and convenient means of servicing the state rooms

Rear elevation of Felbrigg Hall, Norfolk. The wing on the right was added to the early seventeenth century house in the 1670s, and contains two storeys of inter-connecting rooms. The corridor to the left of the wing was added in 1751

Wilton House, Wiltshire, is a sixteenth century courtyard house, which was partly rebuilt in the 1640s. To make the inter-connecting rooms more convenient a corridor was created in the court in 1811

Felbrigg Hall also acquired a corridor which cured the circulation problems within Samwell's late seventeenth century wing. Built 1751 to the designs of James Paine, the two-storey corridor was added to the inner elevation of the L-plan house and so provided independent entry to the ground floor state rooms and upper level bedchambers as well as a route from the kitchen wing to the dining room. A letter of roughly the same date as the additions to Felbrigg reveals the extent to which the late seventeenth century belief that 'the file of rooms' provided 'the prime beauty'[24] of the house had by the mid eighteenth century been replaced by an admiration for convenience. John Carr, writing in 1755 to Edwin Lascelles for whom he was designing Harewood House in Yorkshire, boasted that 'I get into the gallery, bedchamber, dressing room without going through any other room, which seldom can be in such a large house; and have two spacious backstairs of ten feet diameter'.[25]

The corridor, as perfected by Vanbrugh, was one way of providing privacy while retaining parade; another solution grew out of the dramatic change of taste that overtook British architecture in the second decade of the eighteenth century. The fashion for Wren, Vanbrugh and Hawksmoor baroque was eclipsed by a sudden and sustained burst of enthusiasm for the rational and

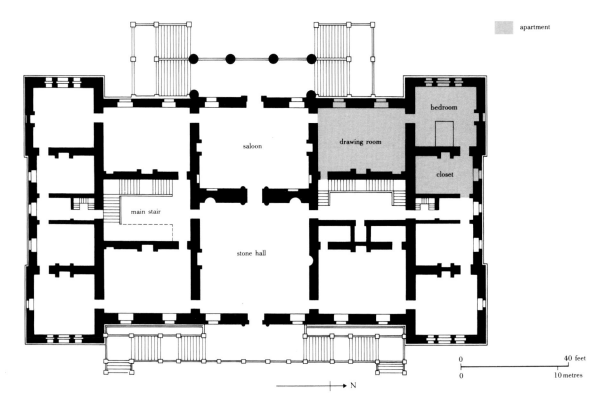

apartment

bedroom

drawing room

closet

saloon

main stair

stone hall

0   40 feet

0   10 metres

N

austere classicism of Palladio. Palladio had previously inspired Inigo Jones, his near contemporaries and followers such as John Webb and Roger Pratt. The starting point for this new revival was a new and careful study of Palladio's buildings. Particularly influential were Palladio's villa plans which demonstrated ways of creating impressive public rooms and convenient private apartments within a relatively modest building. Roger Hooke with Ragley Hall in Warwickshire around 1680 pioneered planning principles that were to be developed more fully by early eighteenth century Palladians.

Ragley has a central axis formed by a hall (room of entry) and a saloon (room for formal dining) around which are arranged four sets of four-room apartments. Each of these apartments, placed symmetrically in the four corners of the first floor, consists of the same room sequence found in an enfilade plan—withdrawing chamber, bedchamber and closet with the useful addition of a servant's bedroom. Dramatic long vistas are still possible across the width of the house, but they possess none of the significance of vistas in an enfilade plan. Instead of indicating the axis of honour within a single apartment, the vistas at Ragley merely look from one apartment into another. The significance of the plan lies in the organisation of the rooms into self-contained apartments and the provision of backstairs which allow each apartment to be entered privately and serviced discreetly.

The *piano nobile* of Houghton Hall, Norfolk, designed by Colen Campbell in the early 1720s and built for Sir Robert Walpole. This floor contains four conveniently planned apartments, each of which could be served discreetly and privately

Houghton Hall in Norfolk was begun in the 1720s and is, in its plan form, a development of the Ragley model. But it is much else beside; indeed, in many ways Houghton is the great monument to the early eighteenth century search for privacy. It was designed by Colen Campbell for Sir Robert Walpole, who made a very lucrative career from being George II's prime minister and who used his money to build a parallel career of being the leading country gentleman in England. Like many of his rich and powerful contemporaries, Walpole sought splendid and idealised isolation. To achieve this at Houghton, he removed the old village from his park and rehoused its inhabitants in two rows of plain uniform cottages that line up outside the main gates to the park, as though queuing for admittance to pay their proper respects.

The exterior of Houghton expresses the primary internal division between

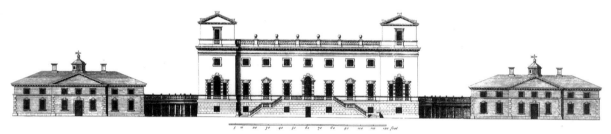

The east elevation of Houghton as designed by Campbell. The façade expresses the primary internal division between public and private worlds with tall windows on the first floor indicating the location of the state rooms

public and private worlds. Modelled on the prototype of the Palladian villa, Houghton possesses a squat ground floor, called the 'rustic' in the eighteenth century, which contained the family rooms and was used for informal entertaining. As Lord Hervey explained soon after the completion of the house, the rustic was the storey dedicated to hunters, hospitality, noise, dirt and business. The first floor, the *piano nobile*, with its pedimented and cornice-capped windows, was the storey dedicated to 'taste, expense, state and parade'.[26]

Within the *piano nobile* there was another balance struck, in the manner of Ragley, between parade and privacy. Here the four apartments arranged (as at Ragley) symmetrically around a hall/saloon central axis, each consist of only three rooms; a withdrawing chamber, a bedchamber and a closet. The pair of apartments each side of the central hall/saloon axis share a service stair which rises near their respective closets. From the point of view of privacy and convenience, this plan represented a significant advance. The compact form of the apartment (compressed by placing the closet at right angles to the bedchamber rather than on its central axis as in the enfilade plan) and the disposition of secondary staircases between closets meant that bedchambers were liberated. They no longer had to serve as through rooms on the route through the state apartments, but could be reached privately from the service

stair. Also and even more important, since each apartment was occupied by a different senior member of the family or by a guest, the rooms flanking the bedchamber were not in common use.

The closets at Houghton were still put to their traditional use. Richly decorated and furnished, they were for intimate meetings or private study or to house collections of curiosities. The closet could also serve more mundane purposes. It could lodge the servant who had to be near at hand to answer the call of the master or mistress. It could also, perhaps simultaneously, lodge the close-stool.

Holkham Hall was another great Norfolk Palladian mansion, designed by Lord Burlington and William Kent who had created the main interiors at Houghton. It was begun in 1734, only a few years after Houghton, and reveals a further advance in the search for privacy and in the separation of uses. Here guest and family bedchambers are placed in separate wings with some servants' bedrooms provided in the kitchen wing. Only two apartments were created in the *piano nobile* of the main block, one of which contained a state bed. Additional and much less formal bedchambers were placed on the second floor of the main block. A generation later, Robert Adam went one better at Kedleston Hall in Derbyshire (built between 1760 and 1765) and gave his clients, Lord and Lady Scarsdale, a family wing to themselves. This was a development which combined the best of both worlds. The family could live in convenient and private accommodation yet entertain and display possessions in splendid state rooms which, out of respect for past fashion, still included a state bedchamber. The family wing, joined to the main house only by a curving corridor, consisted of seven rooms on the *piano nobile* including one bedchamber, a dressing room each and a library for Lady Scarsdale. The remaining rooms were probably for servants and for keeping close-stools and chamber pots.

The fact that the master and mistress of Kedleston chose to share the same bedchamber rather than to have separate rooms seems to reflect a preference shown by most fashionable members of mid-eighteenth century English society. Certainly Sir Watkin Williams-Wynn had a similar set of rooms incorporated in the house Robert Adam designed for him in London's St James's Square (1771). These rooms, arranged as a two-storey rear wing, included two dressing rooms, two powder rooms, one bedchamber, a library (this time for the master), a service stair and two water closets. Adam provided the same rooms, though of different form, for Lord and Lady Derby when he designed their house in Grosvenor Square in 1773.

Necessary purposes

In large country houses built before 1770 evacuating the bowels and washing the body were activities usually carried out within the house. Going to the lavatory could involve no more than reaching for the chamber pot, visiting the close-stool in the closet or a snug little cupboard—of the type shown on eighteenth century plans of Holkham Hall[27] furnished with a seat with a hole in it and a pot beneath that.[28] Bathing could also be a very simple affair, merely involving a servant toiling up the backstairs with buckets of hot water to fill a slipper bath dragged before the bedchamber fire.

In more modest country establishments, it was common to place lavatories in the garden, a location relatively more accessible for their occupants than it would have been for those of mansions. These 'houses of office' were embellished in no mean manner. Rural lavatories were generally earth closets, though a water-flushed system had been developed as early as the 1590s by Sir John Harrington. He made two and presented one to his godmother Queen Elizabeth, who became an instant fan. It did not catch on with other Elizabethans because the technology needed to move vast amounts of sewage and water around was not readily available.

Felbrigg Hall retains a garden lavatory built in 1751, which must be typical of many built during the century. Both its ambitious architectural detail and the interest that William Windham took in fitting it out confirm that this was more than just a servants' lavatory and suggests that hygienic outside lavatories were something of a novelty:

> *Should not the inside be stuccoed? or how do you do it? How many holes? There must be one for the child; and I would have it light as possible. There must be a good place to set a candle on, and a place to keep paper . . . though the better the plainer, it should be neat.*[29]

If something more ambitious was required than a tub of hot water in front of the fire and an earth closet in the garden, then the country-house builder could provide himself with a private water works.

The structure at Carshalton House in Surrey, was built in 1719 for Sir John

(RIGHT) The bath, Carshalton House, Surrey

Fellowes and reveals how far a country house owner had to go in the eighteenth century to get a regular hot bath and running water. This building possessed a water wheel set in an engine room beneath a water tower; a mill stream running beneath the building powered the wheel, and an artificial lake was created between the house and the tower which fed the mill stream. The water wheel pumped water into a lead cistern in the tower which in

The water tower at Carshalton House, was built in 1719 and contains all the apparatus necessary to provide running hot and cold water for a private estate

turn supplied water under pressure to the house and so to a tiled bath at the base of the tower. The building also probably possessed a boiler to heat the water and, for good measure, an orangery to make the most of the hot and clammy conditions.

A similar bathing establishment (now destroyed) was built at Chatsworth. Celia Fiennes described it in some detail in 1697:

ye walls . . . of the batheing room . . . (are) all with blew and white marble . . .

The plunge bath inserted into Wimpole Hall, Cambridgeshire, in the 1790s by Sir John Soane. On the right is an early nineteenth century pillar shower

the bath is one Entire marble all white finely Veined with blew and is made smooth ... It was deep as ones middle on the outside, and you went down steps into ye bath big enough for two people. At ye upper End are two Cocks to let in one hott, ye other Cold water to attemper it as persons please.[30]

Celia Fiennes was clearly intrigued by the novelties of plumbing, for a few years later she recorded a visit to Queen Anne's lavatory at Windsor which was a pioneering example of the water closet: 'Within the dressing room is a closet ... that leads to a little place with a seat of easement of marble with sluices of water to wash it down'.[31]

From the late eighteenth century plunge baths began to appear inside country houses; an excellent example being the bath that Sir John Soane had designed for Wimpole Hall in Cambridgeshire around 1790. But these sorts of bath were still in the tradition of therapeutic spa bathing which had enjoyed its heyday earlier in the century.[32] What was intended for cleansing in the modern sense was the pillar shower standing beside the plunge bath. This shower, which probably dates from the early nineteenth century, provided a quick way of washing that was economical with hot water.

Private baths located near bedchambers did not make a general appearance until the early years of the nineteenth century although, as early as 1664, Samuel Pepys recorded one in the house of a friend in Lincoln's Inn Fields, London.[33] Good, and far more typical early examples, are at Ashridge Park in Hertfordshire, begun in 1806 to the design of James Wyatt. Here bath rooms are located in the family wing, with that for the master of the house being situated conveniently between his study and dressing room.

Life in the modest eighteenth century town house had much in common with life in a great country house. For instance, a house plan common in cities like London and Bath provided for three rooms on each floor. On the upper floors these rooms contained a front drawing room, a rear bedroom and a closet within which (in large-scale terrace houses) a service stair was occasionally located. Perhaps, as at Houghton, each floor was lived in as an apartment belonging to a different member of the family, with even the ground floor rooms containing beds. By 1756 the first floor of the 'common' London house contained, according to Isaac Ware in *A Complete Body of Architecture*, a 'dining-room over the hall or parlour' and 'a bed-chamber ... and closet'. However, Ware was obviously uneasy with the mix of bedroom and living room on the same floor for he continued: 'in a house something better than the common kind, the back room upon the first floor should be a drawing-room, or dressing room, for the lady; for it is better not to have any bed on this floor'. As for the floor above, Ware recorded that 'the two rooms on the second floor are for bed rooms', as was the closet, while the garrets 'may be divided into a larger number (of rooms) than the floor below, for the reception of beds for servants'.

Servants were parcelled out around the house, sleeping not just in garrets but in the basement: 'a bed for a man or two maid servants is contrived to be let down in the (basement) kitchen' wrote Ware. Or they could be accommodated on landings, or sleep on a foldaway bed in the parlour. But, it seems, favoured female servants could share the same bed as their mistress. Pepys records that, while he 'lay in the trundle bed the maid had gone to

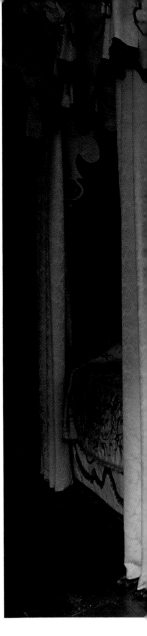

An early eighteenth century urban bed-chamber, created within the second floor front room of 18 Folgate Street, London

bed to my wife',[34] and Daniel Defoe, in his novel *Roxana* published in 1724, makes several references to mistress and maid sharing the same bed when neither happened to have a man staying the night.

Something of the appearance of the town-house bedroom of the first half of the eighteenth century is suggested by an inspired recreation at 18 Folgate Street in east London's Spitalfields. The bedrooms are on the second floor, with the best being the larger front room of the house. This was built around 1725. The bed—a four poster of early eighteenth century style—has its back to the inner wall and faces the windows in the front wall.[35] The smaller bedroom, overlooking the yard, contains a neoclassical couch placed in the

Servants and sensibilities

Until the late eighteenth century the average gentleman's family was entirely dependent on its servants for the smooth running of all aspects of family life from cooking to cleansing, removing slops to dressing. Servants were essential, yet while they had a free run of the entire house, privacy was impossible and blackmail distinctly possible. As Dr Johnson wrote, servants:

> . . . *first invade your table then your breast,*
> *Explore your secrets with insidious art,*
> *Watch the weak hour and ransack all the hearts,*
> *Then soon your ill-paid confidence repay,*
> *Commence your Lords, and govern or betray.*[45]

The tensions caused by servant and family co-inhabiting not only the same floor of the house but also, perhaps, the same room were eased by the general adoption of the wire-operated bell pull. Bell pulls were not unknown before the 1770s, but new technology made them easier and cheaper to install and more efficient.[46] This meant that it was no longer necessary to have servants sleeping around the house within easy call of the family; they could be lodged in separate and distant quarters, to be summoned by bells as needed. This permitted also further development of the ideas we saw emerging at Kedleston. After 1800, country houses began to sprawl in the castellated and asymmetrical manner dictated by the fashion for the picturesque; a form admirably suited for the distant segregation of different occupants of the house. Now not only were family wings usual, but also servants wings, both generally separated by the state rooms. The meandering and castellated Ashridge Park in Hertfordshire is an excellent early example. Built between 1806 and 1817 to the design of James Wyatt, the huge mansion contains not only a central block of state rooms with the family and servants segregated each side in their own wings, but also a kitchen wing, laundry, stables and garden court all forming part of the extended composition.

The spirit of the picturesque also accelerated the final separation in country houses of bedchambers from living rooms. The desire to be close to nature, or at least close to the naturally-landscaped home park and gardens, meant that it became imperative for all who followed fashion to turn as many ground-floor rooms as possible into rooms for entertaining. This meant that beds moved from main floors to upper floors (the state bed at Wimpole was moved upstairs in the 1780s) so that, by 1780 or so, the bedroom had become a very private place indeed; servants no longer had to sleep beside their master or mistress or on the threshhold of their bedchamber and, in larger houses, bedchambers were no longer mixed with rooms in other uses but had finally

Dr Graham's 'marrow melting' Celestial Bed of *c.* 1770, on which Emma Hart—the future Lady Hamilton—displays herself

moved upstairs to create a private community of bedrooms, each entered off a bedroom corridor. The bedroom as we know it, a room of refuge dedicated to sleep and night-time activities, had arrived.[47]

From these same decades of the late eighteenth century comes a reminder that the bed is more than just a piece of furniture for sleeping on. In the 1770s Dr Graham, a notorious quack, invented and marketed his Celestial Bed. This device, an extraordinary sex machine, was located in Graham's Pall Mall chambers, his 'Temples of Health and Hymen' which was presided over by 'Vestina, the Rosy Goddess of health'—a position occupied by young Emma Hart before her transformation into Lady Hamilton.

Emma would lie in a mud bath in the window to attract attention to the

the morals of the nation. It certainly led to even greater privacy, just as did contemporary developments in domestic technologies. New heating systems meant that servants no longer had to toil through the house with scuttles of coal, gas removed the need for servants to fuss over candles or replenish oil lamps and improved plumbing led to the creation of efficient, hygienic and magnificent bathrooms and lavatories which could be run with the minimum of help from the staff.

There were also developments in the bedroom itself; its character as a cosy retreat was strengthened by the addition of all manner of comfortable and useful specialised furniture. Like most rooms in the Victorian house, it reflected that curious characteristic of nineteenth century taste—the horror of unfilled space. Also, in common with other rooms, the bedroom had its doors hinged so as to ensure privacy. As the German architect and writer Hermann Muthesius observed in 1904, one of the Englishman's

> most conspicuous need (is) their desire for privacy, for seclusion . . . the most important point is that people should not be disturbed and this is reflected in the direction in which the door opens. The rule known to every Englishman says that the person entering shall not be able to take in the whole room at a glance but must walk around the door, by which time the person in the room will have been able to prepare himself suitably for this entry.[51]

The bed also underwent a mild revolution in the mid nineteenth century. Just as hangings had tended to give way to timber in the late sixteenth century, now both hangings and timber gave way to metal. The brass bed, a practical piece of hygienic bug-resistant furniture, became almost universal after its virtues were promoted at the Great Exhibition of 1851.

Hygiene, coupled with Victorian philanthropy, highly-tuned morality and reforming zeal, also made privacy possible for the first time for large numbers of the labouring classes. Until the mid nineteenth century, the poor were by and large left to stew in their own misfortune with the Poor Laws providing only very limited relief and that for only the most desperate. The degenerative consequences of the life lived by large numbers of the population had been noted and regretted in earlier times but was, with an air of fatalism, accepted as an unfortunate and unavoidable fact of life. The mid-Victorians introduced a moral dimension. The burgeoning Evangelical wing of the Church of England saw a direct relation between the state of the poor and the state of Christian civilisation. A society which could allow its poor to subsist in conditions that were insanitary and overcrowded, indeed in conditions which led to gross immorality and brutality, was itself in need of help—and it was help that the Evangelicals wanted to give. For the first time the poor found people who were actually willing to buy them privacy. What is arguably the

A late nineteenth century brass bed in Linley Sambourne House, Kensington, London: brass beds were the hygenic riposte to the traditional bug-friendly timber bed with heavy fabric hangings

world's first block of flats built for the urban labouring classes, the class of people who suffered most from overcrowded housing, survives in Holborn's Streatham Street in London. These model dwellings, built in 1849 for the Society for Improving the Conditions for the Labouring Classes, were designed by Henry Roberts, an Evangelical Christian and future adviser to Prince Albert on working-class housing. Roberts, shocked by the 'drunkeness, domestic feuds and vice in its most appalling form' that he saw as the result of overcrowding, described the improvements that he believed his model dwellings would bring about:

> *In providing for the accommodation of a large number of families in one pile of buildings, a leading feature of the plan should be the preservation of the domestic privacy and independence of each distinct family; and the disconnection of their apartments, so as effectually to prevent the communication of contagious disease. This is accomplished by adopting one common open staircase, open on one side to a spacious quadrangle, and on the other side having the outer doors of the several tenements, the rooms of which are protected from draught by a small entrance lobby.*[52]

Stanton Harcourt, Oxfordshire. The medieval
kitchen stands apart from the house in order
to minimise the danger of fire; this is the form
of kitchen that Victorian country house
architects copied over and over and it proved
enduringly practical

CHAPTER THREE

THE
POWER HOUSE

GILLIAN DARLEY

THE AUTHOR WISHES TO THANK THE FOLLOWING FOR THEIR
HELP IN WRITING THIS CHAPTER: LORNA HEPBURN,
ALISON RAVETZ, CAROLINE DAVIDSON AND JOS BOYS.

The power house

Walk into the farmhouse kitchen. Inhale the smell of newly-baked bread, luxuriate in the warmth of the range, feel the hand-made tiles beneath your feet and notice the homely roughness of the wooden plate-rack and the dresser. Never mind if this rural fastness is in the city centre, the bread comes from the supermarket pre-baked, and the range is fired by North Sea gas, the tiles are made in Mexico and the 'unfitted' kitchen conceived at great expense by a bespoke kitchen-design firm. The engine room of the house has, at least for the affluent, become a journey down memory lane, a rustic stage set.

Of course, inside every creaking cupboard door of the urban farmhouse kitchen, sit fellow conspirators. The fridge-freezer, offering freshness at a moment's notice; the dishwasher, quietly carrying on with the housework while the family eats, sleeps or just sits elsewhere; the food processor which cuts, chops and pounds away, making a moment's job out of what once took hours while the washing machine and dryer have replaced the functions of an entire room—the scullery or outside wash-house. There are still dreary, repetitive tasks for women to do, but many of them take seconds or, at most, minutes rather than hours or even days.

The fitted kitchen was a particularly neat way of selling cramped space as newly-built houses became ever smaller. The generous space that the knock-through basement of the terraced townhouse provides in its urban farmhouse kitchen/living room is being emulated on a miniature scale, and at a fraction of the cost, in speculative housing across the country. The desirable kitchen tends to be the star exhibit in the show house, an attainable status symbol dangled in weedling tones by tireless telephone salesmen and women who ring up just as the family sits down to a meal. After all, it comes with the *imprimatur* of those images of ourselves that we receive nightly from the TV screen.

As the kitchen assumes fancy-dress, the language to describe the repetitive business of house-keeping, cooking and washing has assumed its own euphemisms, verbal disguises just as effective as those limed oak doors that hide the fridge-freezer. At school, domestic-science long ago became home-economy, while home cooking seems to be the perogative of pub and restaurant—for at home we are more likely to be reheating precooked dishes,

Interior of the kitchen at Stanton Harcourt, built *c.* 1380, showing ovens of various sizes in the wall

fish and chips or take-away pizza or gourmet dishes from the supermarket freezer cabinet.

In many ways the kitchen *is* the living room. It has taken over from the sitting room as the core of the house and, from having once been the most private of areas—either inhabited by a hard-worked housewife or by bevvies of unseen domestic staff—has become the most public and convivial of all the rooms in the house.

Yet the development of the kitchen as a self-contained room is comparatively recent. More than anything else, it was determined by two essential factors—access to water and ways of producing heat. It began with the outdoor fire of our hunter-gatherer forebears and developed into the central

A Herefordshire farmhouse, photographed in the 1950s, in which the open fire is still being put to good use with an array of hooks and pulleys above. Note the urn hanging permanently over the flame

comfortable all-purpose living room and a back kitchen for wet and dirty operations. There might be a dairy, pantry and brew-house in addition. There were innumerable regional variations—both in function and terminology. In the Lake District the comfortable yeoman farmer would have a 'fire-room' and a 'down-house'—the latter generally used for cooking.

In rural areas, farming families fed themselves through the winter months by smoking meat under the canopy over the main chimney whilst other produce was salted, pickled or dried and then stored in a larder, storeroom or attic. Often a bread oven backed onto the chimney, a practical use for surplus heat. The fire itself was surrounded by contraptions. Pulleys, chain and hooks for the pots that hung above the flame; different kinds of fixing points and devices for turning the spit, as well as the dripping pan below. Great ingenuity was needed to cook a meal in a single pot suspended over the flames, but with tight organisation it proved possible to do by dividing the ingredients with nets—on the pattern of the modern multi-layered steamer.

Before the widespread use of coal (which had been prohibitively expensive, subject to a heavy tax until 1793), all kinds of fuel were pressed into service. Apart from wood, they included peat, bracken, fern and dried dung. In poor

Kitchen hearth, photographed in 1949 in Pembrokeshire, its surplus heat used to smoke hams hanging above, a useful winter food supply before the era of the fridge, deep-freeze and supermarket shopping

V
ki
ar
ch
tv
ra
cc
w
sin
af
m
ki

American Benjamin Thompson, known as Count Rumford, who introduced the pattern of stove which swept Britain in the early nineteenth century.

Rumford designed his system to enclose the heat (most of which had previously been entirely wasted up the chimney), using its radiant qualities and allowing a measure of regulation by means of 'dampers'. He had observed that brick was a better material in which to store heat than iron (a fact widely recognised in Mediterranean countries with their conical, earth-built ovens of great antiquity) and his design took this into account. Nevertheless his name became associated with heavy cast iron ranges which were exactly as wasteful as he had predicted. The oven built into the range added baking to

Yarde Farm, South Devon. A rear view of the house which incorporates a medieval hall house within a number of later changes up to the early eighteenth century

boiling, pot- or spit-roasting as forms of cooking that could be done at home. The range also often incorporated a hot-water boiler and could be used as a warmer for flat irons. It was a marvellous all-purpose work-horse.

Meanwhile, in the well equipped kitchens of large houses, the armies of male household servants were being replaced by a growing fleet of women servants—a process hastened by the levying of a tax on male servants in 1777, to encourage men to join the Navy and to finance the war against American independence. This tax was not repealed until 1937.

Forget the stern, yet golden-hearted butler, rosy-cheeked housekeeper and bevy of willing underlings—the cast of genteel television fiction. The reality of service was a hit-and-miss affair with untrained girls often made unco-operative by long hours and low pay. By 1851, one in every four women in employment was a servant.

Dorothy Wordsworth was unusually lucky with her helper, a 60-year old country woman who, though of limited competence at cooking, was willing, honest and prepared to do washing and ironing. Nor did she take up precious space in the cottage since she went back to her own home at night 'a great convenience in our small house'.

Less cheerful was the portrait that Charles Dickens sketched of the maid who came to blight the first weeks of the young Copperfields' married life. Mary Anne Paragon played upon the innocence and lack of housekeeping skill of Dora the 'child-bride'. 'Our treasure was warranted sober and honest. I am therefore willing to believe that she was in a fit when we found her under the boiler, and that the deficient teaspoons were attributable to the dustman.' Her grim and dishonest personality soon impinged on the newly-married bliss of the couple; eventually she left but was succeeded by a procession of amiable incompetents or thieving no-gooders, including a washerwoman who pawned the clothes. Dickens's fictional cast had innumerable counterparts in Victorian life.

Mrs Beeton's advice, published in her irreplaceable *Book of Household Management* (1861),[5] was aimed at more than one generation of nervous Victorian brides. She likened the running of a home to the task of commanding an army and quoted Oliver Goldsmith 'better a prudent wife or careful matron than a petticoated philosopher or virago queen'. Getting up early, living frugally, avoiding gossip, dressing simply and shopping carefully (unless she has an 'experienced and confidential housekeeper') are recommended. For all her wisdom, Mrs Beeton was only 21 when she began compiling her domestic bible, a year after her own marriage. She was 28 when she died. Isabella Beeton was addressing the swelling middle classes, which is why she made much of economy and living according to your means.

The choice and treatment of domestics was crucially important in Mrs

Beeton's plan of battle, together with regular and careful inspection. The mistress of the house is 'the Alpha and Omega in the government of her establishment ... she is therefore a person of far more importance in a community than she usually thinks she is'. Mrs Beeton had worked out the kind of domestic establishment people on different incomes might expect to run. At the top of the social scale it could consist of 12 male and 13 female servants. At the other end of the spectrum, households subsisting on less than £750 per annum would be unable to employ a man or boy at all (they were an expensive proposition) and would make do with perhaps three maids but more probably with just a single woman servant.

Isabella Beeton, photographed *c.* 1857. Aged only 28 when she died, she had been 21 when she started her Herculean task of telling the Victorian wife how to organise her household

Yet, beyond issuing instructions, the nearest that the wealthiest classes got to the kitchen was the one in the doll's house upstairs in the nursery. Queen Victoria's children went one better, playing in a full-scale kitchen in the Swiss Chalet in the grounds at Osborne House, very possibly their sole contact in life with the regions behind the green baize door.

The Victorians' romanticised view of the medieval had drawn them back to the grand fourteenth century kitchen, a model which they took surprisingly literally and which reappears regularly as a favourite architectural model throughout the mid nineteenth century. The Abbot's Kitchen at Glastonbury, the best known, was copied at least half a dozen times and was published by

Mrs Beeton.[6] The principle was that it had top light and ventilation, a circular layout and a position well removed from the body of the house. It was an eminently practical solution to the problems of catering for enormous numbers of family, guests and staff without interrupting the quite separate business of life in the living quarters of the country house.

Hatherop House in Gloucestershire is just one of the many examples of a Victorian reworking of the medieval kitchen. It dates from 1856 and now makes an ideal school kitchen—as fit to provide the food needed by 240 people daily as for a sizeable Victorian family and its retainers. Top-lit and circular, on the Glastonbury model, it is remarkably practical—even to proving the theory that vaulting would conduct condensation down the walls rather than allowing it to drip down upon the heads of the staff! It has proved so adaptable that it serves the hard-worked couple who cook these days—helped by a phalanx of machines—as well as it did the long-vanished battalions of Victorian indoor staff.

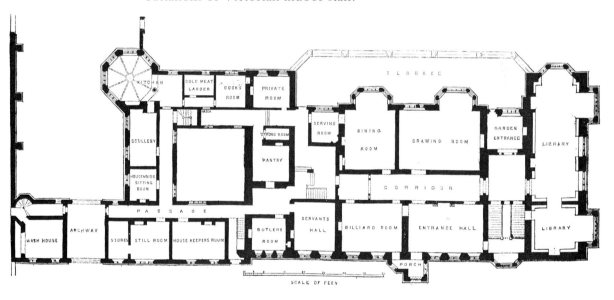

Plan of Hatherop from *The Builder* 1856 showing the labyrinthine journey between the dining room and the kitchen as well as the sequence of rooms in the service end of the house

The Victorians, like their medieval forbears, wanted the kitchen to be segregated—keeping the smells, sounds and large population of the kitchen regions out of sight and mind. The service areas of a large country house were labyrinthine. Robert Kerr's *Gentleman's House*, published in 1864, listed nine separate groups of rooms which made up what he called the 'domestic offices'. These were Kitchen Offices, Upper Servants' Offices, Lower Servants' Offices, Laundry Offices, Bakery and Brewery Offices, Cellars, Storages and Outhouses, Servants' private rooms, Supplementaries and Thoroughfares. There were wet and dry pantries, sculleries, sitting rooms for butler, house-keeper and lesser mortals. The list went on and on. But as far as the family

frying pan and kettle. As the author put it 'the Lambeth woman has no joy in cooking for its own sake'.

While the worst urban conditions were to be found in over-crowded older properties, the pressure was intensifying to provide low-cost, habitable homes for the working class. The Glasgow tenement developed as a particularly neat way of using limited space.[8] The National Trust for Scotland has preserved one which dates from 1892, gaslit and shown as it was found, scarcely altered, in 1970.

The word tends to conjure up slum properties, cramped and badly furnished. But in Glasgow, as in other Scottish cities, people right across the social spectrum lived in tenements. They ranged from one room, or 'single-end' tenement flats right through to those with 10–12 rooms where the wealthy and their servants lived.

The National Trust example is typical of the middle range of tenement. A two room and kitchen flat means that it is one which has four rooms— kitchen, bedroom, parlour and bathroom. As Lorna Hepburn the curator puts it: 'It might be over-crowded by our standards because we tend nowadays to want much more personal space, but certainly wouldn't be over-crowded by the standards of the day'.

A bed in the kitchen is very typical of such Glasgow tenements. High off the ground, very often the space underneath it was used for storage, sometimes even for a tin bath if there was no separate bathroom. Often the parents or the grandmother slept in the kitchen bed. In larger tenements it would be the cook or living-in maid.

The kitchen range, set into the wall and made of cast iron, did far more than just the cooking. Flat irons were heated there, and the washing was hung up to dry on a pulley above. The drawback was that the range was a nightmare to keep clean, needing to be black-leaded at least once a week to prevent it getting rusty or greasy. It needed lots of coal to keep it fired and the coal was kept in a coal bunker on the spot, in the kitchen. 'Imagine the dust rising and landing on all the dishes whenever the coal man came!' notes Lorna Hepburn.

Washing blankets, sheets and larger items was out of the question in a small flat. Here, as in all small, poor homes, only oddments could be washed in the kitchen sink and the main weekly wash was done in a wash-house out in the back court. Each tenant had access to it by strict rota. On the allotted day, the housewife went out at a very early hour in the morning to light a fire underneath the wash copper or boiler. Once the water was heated, the laundry and soap went in and it all boiled away until clean. After that came a thorough rinse, wringing with a mangle or wringer and then the wash had to be hung out to dry. If it was raining, everything had to be brought indoors

fully resolved until the Thirties, and the lethal festoons of wires which accompanied the toasters and other devices of the automated kitchen were neither sightly nor safe, the genie of the modern kitchen had appeared. The threat posed by gas had sparked off the electricity industry's product ranges, but nevertheless cost remained a major obstacle as far as appliances fuelled by either were concerned. Even in the 1920s, after wide expansion into the domestic market, gas still cost five times as much as coal. A refrigerator cost £80 in 1930, at a time when the average weekly wage was £5.

The restrictions and rigours of Victorian domesticity had bred their own reaction. For social reformers with women's rights in mind, freedom was the kitchenless house. The first architect designed co-operative home was illustrated in the *Building News* in 1874 and the Ladies Residential Chambers Limited came into existence in 1888 to build and manage blocks of flats designed around a communal dining room,[10] relieving the young professional women living there of the burden of domestic chores.

For a few years around the turn of the century radical thinkers such as Ebenezer Howard, the founder of the garden city movement, energetically promoted the idea of the co-operative dwelling with common dining room and kitchen. Mrs Howard herself was treated to life in a kitchenless flat at Letchworth, an arrangement her husband felt would 'wisely and effectively utilise a little of this vast volume of now-wasted woman's ability and woman's energy'. H. G. Wells supported this point of view, writing in *A Modern Utopia*, that 'the ordinary Utopian would not more think of a special private kitchen for his dinners than he would think of a private flour mill or dairy farm'.

Mary Broad's experience of life at Waterlow Court in Hampstead Garden Suburb dated from the 1930s, when the co-operative experiment had begun to break down, even though the communal dining room was still in operation. Now in her nineties, she remembers the pioneering women whom she met when she came to live there: 'They were very fine women and they were quite formidable to me, I was young and rather afraid of them but not for long. I got to appreciate their quiet sort of self-confidence'.

The tiny scullery provided in the flat itself was fitted out for little more than the means to make a hot-water bottle or tea or coffee; everything else was available down in the dining room. 'Well, it was rather nice, I mean you just said what you wanted, whatever meal you wanted, and it came, and it was always beautifully cooked and the room was always looking very charming and we all met one another'. Of course the liberation from repetitive chores that the young professional women enjoyed only meant that someone else had to be paid to do them. Mary Broad had her own maid

The promise offered by electricity seemed boundless, or so the manufacturers claimed. Modern GEC would be hard-pressed to offer a single domestic item which could perform this many tasks. (From the *Illustrated London News*, 30 June, 1928)

The new breed of independent professional women, portrayed in the early 1900s at Waterlow Court, Hampstead Garden Suburb, designed along co-operative lines, with a communal dining room and cooked meals provided at the end of a working day

who came in to help out. It was a somewhat illusory state of affairs. Now those tiny sculleries have been converted back into miniaturised kitchens.

Even in large new country houses, electricity and modern appliances were taking their share of the burden and the numbers in the servants' quarters were dropping inexorably. Castle Drogo in Devon was begun in 1910 and not completed until 1927, when the family moved in—just four years before the client, Julius Drewe, died.

But, despite the intervention of the First World War and innumerable other structural and financial problems, Sir Edwin Lutyens carried on building a twentieth century castle and used his usual ingenuity to incorporate any available domestic technology, including hydro-electricity supplied by the local river. His modernity did not however extend to listening to his client's wife. For the kitchen, Mrs Drewe asked for more natural light for her cook ('a glint of sun'). Sir Edwin said distemper would do and it remained top-lit, on the medieval model.

Castle Drogo, Devon, designed by Edwin Lutyens with enormous attention to practical detail as well as overall visual impact. Behind it lies the Victorian passion for the central, top-lit medieval kitchen, but here indulging Lutyens' Arts and Crafts inspired love of materials

There was still a complete and separate world below stairs, consisting of numerous rooms ancillary to the main kitchen. They were all designed with Lutyens' particular touch, blending highly skilled craftsmanship in the best available materials with ergonomic efficiency. The scullery had architect-designed plate racks, draining boards, a gargantuan pestle and mortar and hexagonal chopping block—but also a lift which took food up to the servants' hall as well as the nurseries at the top of the house. The larder was designed not only with traditional slate shelving but also around the well, for added coolness, and with a special vegetable rack into which garden produce could be conveniently pushed, from the garden.

The pantry, with its own sink, was lined with cupboards for china and also housed the bellboard and telephone exchange—representing both the ancient and modern means of communication between one part of the house and another. On plan it is clear that the pantry was the pivot, linking the kitchen wing and the dining room via a service corridor.

Lutyens' own picture of a kitchen was a good deal closer to that of the romantic water-colourist than to the practising cook. It was, he wrote, a room where 'the pots and range glisten in the light, where a cheery cook turns mountains into molehills and frugal fare into a feast'. Nevertheless the kitchen boasted two fine coal-fired ranges, so perhaps the cook *was* relatively cheerful.

The English kitchen was rarely a seedbed for innovation. Its role was far more that of a storehouse of tradition—whether that tradition was embodied in the hearth or in the social order. When Hermann Muthesius reported on English domestic architecture around 1900 in his three volumed *Das Englische Haus*[11] he noted a number of characteristics, expressed in the organisation of houses large and small, which deviated from the continental practice.

He observed the rigid separation of food preparation (dry work) from all kinds of cleaning (wet work). As he put it, 'even in the smallest cottage the English kitchen is unthinkable without its attendant scullery'. Another oddity Muthesius noted was the English insistence on burying the range in an alcove—commemorating the traditional hearth—rather than allowing it to be free-standing. So impossible was it that 'every French chef who comes to England declares that he cannot possibly prepare even the simplest sauce on such a medieval contraption'. He remarks disapprovingly that 'so inseparably bound up with the English notion of an interior is it that they still want to create the impression of a fire-place in their kitchens'.

The English fondness for the open fire was also important because of the toasting of bread 'so important an element of the English breakfast' as well as our liking, which he shared, for simple roast meat, unencumbered by sauce. He described and illustrated the bottle-jack, a contraption which turned the meat mechanically behind a meat screen in front of an open fire, a more

class women began to be more comparable. Many working-class families found themselves comfortably housed in well-designed council housing while middle-class women, who had been accustomed to a life with servants throughout childhood, had almost at a stroke to learn how to look after their families themselves. Lives which had formerly been poles apart inevitably became similar. The differences tended to be those of small degree—such as the handy labour-saving devices that the middle-class housewife could afford to buy. She could also help herself by unloading some of the most labour-intensive tasks that a maid servant would have been required to carry out. Black-leading iron stoves and weekly cleaning of the flues, the endless bleaching and starching of linen and whitening of door steps were dispensed with and other jobs were simplified by, for example, lacquered brasswork or replacing metal door furniture with a porcelain or painted equivalent.[13]

Out in the suburbs, in a new house, the young wife was planning what to do with her day. In the 1930s, despite the Depression, she was unlikely to have a maid although she might have a part-time 'help'. She needed advice and her best source of practical assistance came in the guise of columns in new women's magazines or in publications specifically targeted at her and her kind, such as the *Daily Express* publication *The Home of Today*.[14]

According to the latter volume, she should embark on her day at 6.30am—only thirty minutes later than Mrs Beeton had suggested that the housewife set about her business. Tasks for the week included cooking and shopping for three meals a day, turning out one room each day, a moment to 'review the larder' and three hours in the afternoon for 'personal requirements, social engagements etc'. Her family might be persuaded to help with the final tasks of the day, including 'wash up, prepare tray for breakfast and dining-room for morning work'. If from time to time she felt like a hamster on a treadmill, it was hardly surprising.

No wonder the housewife needed labour-saving ideas such as the serving hatch and the invaluable, prettily named 'hostess trolley'. Other innovations such as enamelled and tiled surfaces made cleaning easier, while if she was fortunate, the demon coal dust might be confined to a fire in the living room. Her cooking would be done by gas or electricity, though the latter was still far behind in the race for supremacy. Sinks, cupboards and shelving were better designed and made of modern materials which could be easily wiped down, rather than requiring a hard scrub. Even so, the plethora of new equipment introduced the prospect of new and awful tasks, including some as seemingly futile as vacuuming the bed springs.

Organisations like the promotional Electrical Development Association and the more educational Electrical Association for Women (founded in 1924) whipped up the excitement, ensured plenty of interest and helped to sell the goods. The inherent contradictions in apparently labour-saving equipment were still not fully revealed. As Jos Boys put it:

> *I think it's quite difficult for us to appreciate the sort of power that the idea of domestic science had for women, this idea that you could . . . professionalise housework, that it was like being in a laboratory. And that it could be rationalised and that you could work out the whole series of tasks that women did, and that you could organise the kitchen so that it was so small that you could do it all standing on one spot.*

As the house became a more sophisticated, internally serviced unit so the building costs rose. By the 1930s, cheaper speculative housing had to compete with the advances made at the upper, architect-designed end of the market, often years before. Those who were buying the new houses in the suburbs which were growing on the fringes of the major cities, were being innundated by the imagery promoted and advertised in women's magazines and in the press. As John Burnett has written '. . . the functionalists misread the times. People did not want "a machine for living in" so much as a vehicle for living out a fantasy'.[15] With smaller families and with life centred upon the home itself, the preoccupation with the immediate domestic surroundings was an engrossing if entrapping, affair.

The economies that the builders had to make, in order to provide the equipment to which the purchaser aspired, meant in the end economies of space. Yet a small space need not be a cramped space, so long as it is efficiently and ergonomically designed for the purpose. Innovation came, for example, from work on the design of caravans and later from the prefabricated houses produced in the immediate postwar years by the munitions factories, newly geared up to manufacture the temporary housing needed following the widescale devastation of German bombing raids.

That postwar sense of urgency and technical confidence benefited kitchen design, as indeed it did the entire construction business. Show houses included items such as gas wash coppers (the traditional terminology lingered on), the stainless steel sink unit and the electric cooker—now a neat, well designed piece of equipment. By the 1950s the electric washing machine was making headway, soon to be followed by spin and tumble dryers. The speed with which the domestic washing machine was adopted—in 1948 less than four per cent of households in Britain had one, by 1980 the figure was 77 per cent and rising[16]—reflects the understandable desire of the housewife, particularly the one with small children, to be rid of the ceaseless grind of hand washing.

While those who were selling houses concentrated on the number of domestic appliances and the modernity of the fittings, the committees (by then including a number of women) which drew up the housing standards

Heath Robinson's version of the economies of space needed in a bungalow. In fact the advances in design to make the kitchen of a caravan, prefab. or even aircraft, ergonomically sound were soon shared by the public

(TOP) Bleached oak farmhouse kitchen somewhere in south-west London—a favourite image for the 1980s. (ABOVE) Graphite and stainless steel, the pristine shape of the modern kitchen. (OPPOSITE) A true farmhouse kitchen, never blessed by the intervention of a kitchen designer, in which all the daily work of the farm goes on as well as the usual domestic tasks for the family. Part of the medieval house, it still remains its centre

manuals for the public sector were more concerned about whether it was preferable to design a kitchen with an eating area or alcove or to continue to banish the whole business to another room, perhaps now linked by a hatch.

The advent of the TV supper (a meal served on a tray and eaten in an armchair) as well as the kitchen breakfast bar whether demountable or fixed has broken down much of the rationale for these demarcations. Even so, what we call the spaces into which we divide domestic life and how we use them offer a curious mingling of the symbolic and the nostalgic—and nowhere is this more evident than in the kitchen. Never mind that much of the presentation is hinged upon marketability rather than on social *mores*, the walls between rooms are crumbling as slowly and surely as those between the sexes. As Jos Boys says: 'It's to do with whether the cooking of food is something that's somehow private and separate, as it was when servants did it or whether it's part of everyday life, part of the family living and working together'. The modern kitchen cum living room reflects our acceptance of that.

For the unfortunate dispossessed, confined to a marginal world of bed-and-breakfast and hostel accommodation and, by the standards of our time, probably considerably less well provided-for than many a poor Victorian family, the lack of anywhere at all to cook—let alone a kitchen—is homelessness's ultimate insult.

As the Victorians retreated into a dream world from which the kitchen re-emerged as a hive of activity, and the Edwardian new woman aspired to life without a kitchen sink, we luckier *second* Elizabethans retreat into different versions of highly mechanised rusticity or state of the art modernity.

The kitchen as laboratory and the farmhouse kitchen both have historical antecedents and equally represent illusion rather than reality. Whether the oven used to cook the family Sunday lunch is a fan-assisted electric model made by a smart German manufacturer or a modern cast-iron range, offering the advantages of its Victorian forebear whilst being conveniently fuelled by gas, oil or electricity, the truth is that the operations in a kitchen equipped to modern standards vary little; it is only a matter of cosmetic disguise.

In the real farmhouse kitchen, floors get astonishingly muddy, meals cannot be delayed, there is no deviation from routine whether that is dictated by animals or by the family. The farmer's wife still has an arduous and insistent timetable, nowadays probably complicated by school runs and meetings with reps and accountants, as well as the inevitably long list of tasks around the farm. The urban farmhouse kitchen store cupboard might contain a pot or two of home-made marmalade alongside preserved produce from all over the world; there may be some herbs growing on the window sill or out on the patio in a tub, but true resemblances stop there.

While the country style kitchen diverts us towards one kind of muddled but harmless dream world, the design-conscious kitchen of recent years seems to me to offer an equally dishonest—but less comfortable—mirage.

Here the gleaming steel, the pristine glass, the crisply remodelled kitchen furniture, are all promising scientific modernity, but at what a cost! Meticulous cleaning of black, white or matte steel surfaces is *de rigeur*, a labour-intensive martyrdom to good taste. You only take this path if someone else is going to do the work.

Ostentatious modernity is little more than a designer garment. The computer-programmed oven, electronic remote control and robotic cooking have not progressed very far beyond the pages of science fiction. In the absence of genuine technological advance, which might in reality lessen the tyranny of domestic drudgery, a new tyranny has stepped in—that of style.

Whether sold down the phone at the cheapest end of the market or marketed from air-conditioned premises at a 'good' address with a pseudo-professional kitchen designer sitting on a high stool in front of a drawing board or VDU, the kitchen is one area for which women are the indisputable decision-makers and spenders. A highly lucrative market has been infinitely expanded by the subtle insinuation that your kitchen is a personal status symbol—by their kitchens shall ye know them.

Yet comfortable disorder, which is the reality of the all-purpose kitchen/living area, reflects the choice of many working women, the near-impossible juggling of roles and tasks. An average early evening might include cooking, loading then unloading the washing machine, keeping an eye on the children and animals, catching up on correspondence or paperwork, casting an eye at the TV around newstime—and that's just a fraction of the day. This is a room in which everything (and everyone) must be visible and within easy reach. Forget the aesthetics, long live ergonomics.

Of course, men are back in the kitchen nowadays—and if anyone is in doubt then that litmus test of social change the television commercial tells us nightly that it is so. Now that the worst of the drudgery has gone they are happy enough to cook or do the washing up, although men are still rarely seen ironing, mopping the kitchen floor or unloading the washing machine. Scullery work, wet work, is still women's work.

As now perfected, the kitchen is the temple of the late twentieth century professional homemaker. The wages for housework campaign raised the issue of what she is up to, and just how much she is expected to do, but provided no answers to the questions it raised. The status symbol kitchen is really just a tranquilliser, even a placebo, soothing the housewife as she continues to perform a hundred tedious and repetitive tasks accompanied by her biddable domestic staff, those whirring appliances and pounding machines that keep her company all day long.

The pop-artist as prophet. Richard Hamilton's
1956 painting *Just what is it that makes today's homes
so different, so appealing* presents a surreal foretaste
of the world of consumer durables to come

CHAPTER FOUR

THE ELECTRONIC COTTAGE

MARTIN PAWLEY

So different, so appealing?

'Jeepers creepers wouldn't you like to own a home like this?' runs the full page advertisement. It is for a new but vaguely Edwardian-looking terraced house in what Barratt the Builders called its Premier Collection 'at prices from just £20 000 right up to £500 000.' At one time, as you may recall, something at the '. . . right up to' end in Dulwich was owned by a Mrs Thatcher, of Westminster; but this is one of the cheaper ones intended for the younger set, with a four-wheel drive jeep parked outside and props to suggest that the gang has all been waterskiing.

Another advertiser tries a different tack. 'Fifty years ago one of the best cameras available might have cost around 15 guineas and this very substantial new Costain home fetched just over £450. Now a flash-bang up-to-date camera is around the £400 mark and a new Costain home? Anything from £28 000 to £250 000.' This advertisement shows a 1935 vest-pocket Kodak camera and a creditable copy of a Lutyens villa of the same period, matched with a Nikon F-501 and a new end-of-terrace house with fake leaded lights and no chimney.

Much lower down the ladder, buried in the middle of an advertisement feature, we find Caroline and Adrian who have just purchased their first home—a Laing 'Pimlico' one bedroom apartment. 'We see our first home very much as the move along a property-owning path which will lead to gradually bigger and better homes as the years go by' intones Adrian as though reading from a script. 'We are very well aware that unless you start early, you have no hope of joining this all-important chain of owning properties (sic), which appreciate in value and give you the chance to steadily improve your living standards.' There is a picture of Adrian, and Caroline too, looking somewhat less brainwashed than they sound, outside their 'Pimlico'. Significantly the caption reads: 'The spacious apartment has its own front door'.

Clearly Adrian and Caroline, the waterskiing gang, Mrs Thatcher and the camera club were all deeply into the 1980s housing market—but did any of them really understand what made it go or what it really meant? Did any one of them even wonder why all the new houses in those 1986 advertisements looked so old-fashioned?

It was no good searching for the answers in the magazines that flooded

The Laing 'Pimlico' one bedroom maisonette block c.1986 with 'Caroline and Adrian' admiring their own front door. The small apartment building is designed to look like a detached house

onto the market during the great property boom. They seldom ventured into anything more philosophical than interior decorating, insurance, mortgage finance and law. There the sky was the limit. 'This is not the place to question the relative merits of one form of construction or another' as one editorial sandwiched between mortgage broker advertisements put it. 'It is more appropriate to point out how house styles and finishes have improved. It's almost like buying a new car, as soon as you have bought the current model, there is a better, faster, bigger one on the market'.

That, in a nutshell, was what all the new home builders of the 1980s wanted homeowners to believe, so they produced new houses consisting of serviced floorspace enveloped by investor-readable features. Their uncertainly traditional appearance chiefly the result of the application of straight lines to items such as dormer windows, hipped roofs, gable ends, exposed timbers and overhanging first floors—the kinds of features that, when they were used in the vernacular building of two centuries and more ago, were heavy, irregular, sagging and bent, not thin, spindly and straight.

The resurrection of these features from the scrapyard of architecture was not part of a massive yearning for authenticity; it was part of the massive effort made by the booming housing credit industry to provide itself with a long and glorious past. For all of these things are associated with the timeless values that hot money is not. If this were not so, builders would have gone—and might still go—to greater lengths to get things right. As it is, the absence of a chimney is a dead giveaway for a modern house, even in the middle of one of those exclusive developments modelled on sets for Robin Hood. And there are other clues; concrete pantiles, too regular and too steeply pitched to ever look like their Roman originals; Georgian sash lookalike windows that are actually top-hung; fanlights let into front doors instead of standing above them; precision synthetic slates, all exactly the same colour; brick-on-edge lintels actually resting on steel behind; precision bull's eye panes of glass, every one dead centre; fake leaded lights; lever door handles instead of round knobs; glistening resin-coated woodwork; gratuitous bits of tile-hanging, clapboarding and rendering; galvanised vents puncturing roofs; ornate bits of black-painted ironwork supporting plastic planters.

Apart from being historically wrong—which is not really important because these assemblies of features would be no better as functional modern homes even if the period details were right—these houses all have something else in common. They have been minimalised. Whether they are built with brick and concrete block cavity walls (so-called 'traditional construction'—even though this tradition does not yet ante-date living memory), or with separate brick and wooden stud skins (so-called 'timber-frame con-struction')—even though there is no reason why a timber-frame house should have a brick skin around it), they are all designed to use the thinnest possible walls and the smallest possible amounts of building material. This is not in itself a criticism, for the thermal performance of these houses—thanks to extremely non-traditional insulation materials as well as the plastic mem-branes and double glazing concealed about them—is far higher than was ever achieved, or even tried for, in the past. In the days of the roaring open fire, heat loss was prodigious but there was no problem of condensation, water vapour pressure, radon gas build-up, formaldehyde fumes or mere lack of oxygen. Snug as they are, the atmosphere inside a 'Braemar', a 'Cheviot', a 'President' or an 'Executive' in the winter is more like a Boeing 747 at 40 000 feet than any advertisement stressing traditional values would lead you to believe.

But these technological compromises with history are not the real penalties of minimalisation. In houses as in yachts, the designer always strives for

The evolution of multi-functional space in small houses. This 600 square foot 'cellular' three bedroom bungalow plan of 1904 (a) has no kitchen—cooking was done on the range in the living room. The open planned 1000 square foot three bedroom bungalow of 80 years later (b) has unobstructed space flowing from the hall, through the lounge, dining and kitchen areas on to a covered terrace. Finally, in the 200 square foot single-person 'Microflat' (c) only the bathroom and the hall can be isolated from one universal cooking, living, working and sleeping space

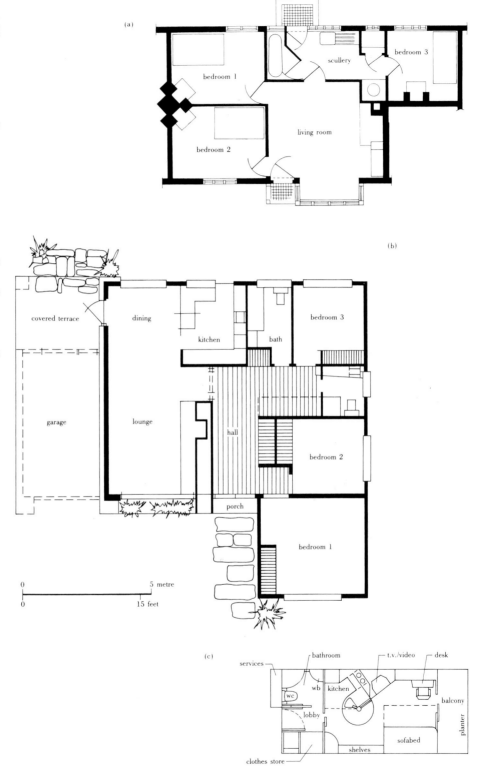

(a)

bedroom 1

bedroom 2

scullery

bedroom 3

living room

(b)

covered terrace

dining

kitchen

bath

bedroom 3

garage

lounge

hall

bedroom 2

porch

bedroom 1

0   5 metre

0   15 feet

(c)

services

bathroom

t.v./video

desk

wb kitchen

wc

balcony

lobby

planter

clothes store

shelves

sofabed

comfort, performance and price and always end up with two of them at the cost of the third. The real impact of miniaturisation in housing is to be found in the way its physical footprint has shrunk to the barest minimum consistent with the claim that the features it is advertised to possess are actually present. Bedrooms in some new homes are so small that they fail to meet not only the Parker Morris space standards of the 1960s, but even the space standards recommended by the Tudor-Walters report of 1918. According to the housing committee of the Institute of Environmental Health Officers, some second bedrooms in new houses are only 40 square feet in area and show houses on new estates are actually fitted out with undersized furniture to make them look bigger. Starter homes in the London area can be as small as 260 square feet and, if they are larger than 350 square feet (including the floor areas of uninhabitable cupboards of course), the builder boasts about 'not

Stacking modular prefabricated hotel bedrooms by crane. This technique played a part in the genesis of the single-person dwelling 'Microflat'

having to fold away double beds' and being able to fit a cooker, a fridge/freezer *and* a washing machine into the kitchen.

At first sight these sizes may not appear extreme. Robert Kerr, one of the founders of the Architectural Association, designed a high-density tenement in 1866 that squeezed a large number of four-person households into 340 square foot apartments by means of built-in folding beds. Using a mezzanine floor in starter home style, D.G. Hoey got the four-person limit for a

Computer graphic simulation by architect Robert Barnes of 96 'Microflats' assembled into a 'singles' apartment building

tenement apartment down to 187 square feet in 1889. But none of the ingenious Victorian pioneers had to include modern domestic appliances, and all of them provided communal wash-houses and lavatories instead of fitted kitchens and private bathrooms. The modern starter homes designer has a smaller household to deal with, but a lot more machinery to get into the allotted space.

About a century after Robert Kerr and D.G. Hoey—and five years after the advent of the 260 square foot starter home—another prototype mini-dwelling made its debut. Adapted from a metal shipping container that had itself been developed into part of a modular steel lift shaft, the 200 square foot Microflat was the brainchild of designer John Prewer, who trained as an architect during the ascendancy of Modern ideas and subsequently studied the prefabrication of houses in Japan. Prewer based his Microflat on simple container technology allied to sophisticated automobile industry standards of fitting out. To that formula he added a knowledge of demographic predictions that showed him exactly why the size of the average dwelling is bound to decrease even as the number of separate dwellings increases.

Intended primarily for stacking up and concreting into position to provide instant blocks of flats, Microflat was also touted for a number of other innovative accommodation uses including student housing, overflow hotel rooms, rooftop *pieds-à-terre*, and (opportunistically) 'slot-in' living accommodation for the instant conversion of unlettable office blocks. Though internally ingenious, with its interior designed as one single, continuous flowing space by car industry consultants Styling International, the Microflat was by no means the first dwelling pod to be promoted as the home of the future. Notionally priced at £28 000 in 1990, a production line Microflat would undoubtedly cost more today—but then it has quite a margin to exploit before it catches up with the price of a conventional starter home.

Appropriately for the way we live now, the steel and plastic prototype contained £10 000 of state of the art electronic communications equipment; an aircraft-style vacuum toilet; low-voltage lighting; a heat recovery system for energy efficiency, and a patented double bedsettee for comfort. Its shower and mini kitchen were specially designed to occupy the minimum space while providing the maximum ergonomic convenience. These features apart, the only really remarkable thing about it was Prewer's marketing decision to abandon any pretence that its purpose was anything other than single person accommodation. Conceptually this was a breakthrough because it corresponded to social realities, instead of the social wish-fulfillments generally peddled in connection with such dwellings as the 'Pimlico' in the small homes market during the 1980s.

Consciously or unconsciously, the design of the Microflat accepts that there is a connection between the automation of the home and the fragmentation of family and community life. One out of three marriages in Britain ends in divorce, and divorce is one of the most often cited causes of house sales. But it is really a cause, or an effect? By the year 2002, of the 1.7 million new households formed in the United Kingdom, 1.3 million of them will be singles, half of them retirees. The other 800 000 will be singles between the age of 30 and 65. Come war or recession, boom or bust, this new housing market for singles is a demographic certainty.

Do we all secretly want to live alone? Or is there nothing secret about it? One hundred and fifty years ago the average Victorian household numbered 5.8 persons; the average household today comprises 2.1. Soon it will dip below 1.9 and we shall begin to understand the true anti-social purpose of all the labour-saving technology with which we have filled our houses and our lives. We shall begin to suspect the hidden agenda of the car that frees us from public transport only to tie us up alone in traffic jams; the meaning of the supermarket that saves us from having to cook; the washer-dryer that frees us from the laundrette; the freezer that cuts us loose from shopping hours; the fax and telephone that give us 'distance working' and save us from having to go to the office and meet all the people we don't want to see; the answerphone that saves us from having to speak to the people we don't want to talk to; the stereo and the television that stop us from having to listen to ourselves; the video recorder that frees us from programme times at the cinema and television schedules . . .

In this way the Microflat, no more than a large and complex consumer durable for living in, reveals the social destination of all consumer durables. This single person box, crammed with as much technology as a fighter plane, represents the logical end of the miniaturisation of the housing market. Whatever its commercial fate, it really is the generic home of tomorrow; offering a level of privacy and isolation that previous generations would have considered pathological.

For all their willing service, the machines of consumer society have exacted a price. That price has been the destruction of the ancient mutual dependency that made us into a cohesive community hundreds of years ago and generated the image of home that we still fanatically defend today, even though its reality has gone forever.

But if the machine-produced single person dwelling is to be the housing solution of the twenty-first century, the definitive house of the twentieth century is something else. Neither an industrial product like a car, nor a professionally hand-crafted artefact like the homes of previous centuries— however closely it may resemble them in appearance—the ordinary twentieth century suburban dwelling is the uniquely popular creation of our time. Neither large nor fashionable but small, ubiquitous, old and new at the same time, its origin and development is a microcosm of the history of the century that is now speeding to its close.

Fanfare for the common man

The story of the twentieth century house begins with housing and ends with homes. It all starts with the Great War, the First World War of 1914–1918. Until then home ownership as we know it scarcely existed. More than 90 per cent of the houses, flats and tenements in Britain were rented out by private landlords on terms ranging from long leases to 'at will'—the latter meaning that the occupants could effectively leave, or be evicted, on a week's notice. In those days the homes of ordinary people bore a uniform aspect, more like the Microflat than the flamboyant 'Premier' or the 'Pimlico', with whole streets of houses in the ownership of a single landlord, all their front doors and window frames painted in a single colour, and all maintained to the standard of repair established by the landlord. With the coming of the Great War this system, whose origins can actually be traced back beyond feudal times to the ancient world, came to a sudden end.

In 1914 Britain sent an expeditionary force to fight the Germans in France. Among the consequences of this commitment was the suddenly urgent need to expand the armed forces enormously. The demands which total war made upon the population transformed the rental market in housing. New housebuilding virtually ceased, but troop concentrations and the needs of the munitions industry created an immense demand for accommodation. Soon soaring rents led to widespread evictions and growing unrest. Riots and rent strikes started in Scotland and spread across the country. The government was forced to act. A law was passed that ultimately created today's owner-occupier housing market: the Increase of Rent and Mortgage (War Restrictions) Act 1915.

Because it was retrospective, requiring landlords to freeze their rents (and mortgage lenders their interest rates) at the figures current at the outbreak of war, the effects of this measure were incalculable. Government assurances that market rents would return at the end of hostilities seemed increasingly unrealistic as the war continued. When the war finally did end in November 1918 retail prices were 225 per cent higher than they had been in 1914. Only one thing could stifle the pressure for a massive postwar increase in rents— the prospect of a repeat of the 1917 Russian Revolution if four million trained soldiers returned to civilian life only to find their rents twice as high as when they went away.

Graph of new house completions, all sources 1860-2000

homes in thousands

years in decades

Source: Central Statistical Office. Annual abstract of statistics

A simplified graph of housing output in the UK 1860–2000. The 'stop/go' effect of the two World Wars and the two post-war recovery booms is striking

The result was the 'Homes fit for heroes' election of December 1918 in which a Liberal government was returned to power on a pledge to construct 500 000 new houses in three years, the houses to be let at subsidised rents by local authority landlords. For the time being, the controlled rents of millions of existing houses, flats and tenements with sitting tenants were to remain at 1914 values.

During the years that followed, these rent-controlled dwellings trickled, flowed and finally flooded out of rental into ownership and a great revolution in tenure took place. Although a million new controlled-rent council houses were built before the outbreak of the Second World War in 1939, more than three times as many privately rented dwellings shifted into owner-occupation during the same period. Landlords, in despair at rent controls that had turned their assets into liabilities, sold their investment properties to tenants at knockdown prices.

It is estimated that in 1914 there were no more than 750 000 owner occupiers out of 7 750 000 households in the United Kingdom. By 1938 there were 3 750 000 out of 11 750 000. Rent control was a blow from which the landlords never recovered, for it was applied again to all new rented property at the outbreak of the Second World War in 1939 and was not effectively repealed for another 30 years.

Between 1914 and 1950 Britain was at war for the equivalent of one day out of every three and a half, and during the second great struggle Britain's housing suffered even more cruelly from the effects of neglect, aerial bombardment and want of new construction than it had in the first. By 1945 no less than 450 000 houses had been destroyed by bombs and over three million

were listed with the War Damage Commission as having suffered damage of some kind as a result of enemy action; concurrently, nearly six years of normal peacetime housebuilding had been lost.

This time, even before the end of the war, plans were made for a national housing effort that would more than make good the deficit. The entire economy had been mobilised to win the war and it was proposed to apply the same principles to solving the housing problem. The 1940–45 wartime coalition government requested the munitions industries to develop designs

Arcon 'prefabs' at Great Yarmouth in 1946. These mass-produced dwellings were designed for a life of ten years while permanent housebuilding caught up after the war

for emergency factory-made houses or 'prefabs' intended to last ten years, of which half a million were to be manufactured in the first postwar year and as many as necessary thereafter. At the same time it was intended that the inter-war local authority role in providing new rental housing would be greatly expanded, and a form of licensing was introduced to guarantee priority for the public sector in the allocation of all building materials and skilled labour.

In the event, these plans proved over-ambitious. Within two years of the end of the war a balance of payments crisis led to a switch in resources from housing to exports. Only 170 000 of the advanced-technology, state-financed prefabs were completed before the programme was cancelled in 1947, although they were to remain popular for many years with their fully-finished interiors and high level of equipment, and many have survived for three times their projected lifespan. By chance one of them was allocated to the parents of the future Labour Party leader, Neil Kinnock. In 1986 he remembered: 'It had a fitted fridge, a kitchen table that folded into the wall and a bathroom. Family and friends came visiting to view the wonders. It seemed like living in a spaceship'. ('When I was a child' *Daily Mail* September 26th 1986).

In addition to the prefabs, one million permanent local authority dwellings were built between 1945 and 1951 (when the postwar Labour government lost power) and this doubling of the public sector estate had an important political effect. From then on the Labour Party began to look to council tenants to form the core of its voting support.

Not only did the production of local authority housing match or exceed the production of private housing until the late 1960s, but the new experimental approach to the design and production of housing begun during the war led to a generation of 'utopian' public sector planning and housing projects that included whole New Towns as well as large citadel-like council estates. For the first time housing design was in the hands of 'experts', as opposed to builders and private developers. As a result, architects and prefabrication specialists, heavily influenced by the concrete system-building techniques developed in Scandinavia and Eastern Europe, conceived whole high-rise cities with 'streets in the air'. Two vast Sheffield council estates, Park Hill and Hyde Park, typified this approach, with more than 10 000 individual dwellings combined into vast concrete slab blocks arranged like dominoes across the landscape. In the same way rows of 27-storey tower blocks were erected to replace the infamous Gorbals slums in Glasgow.

The most ambitious ideas for the advancement of this new form of housing came right at the end of the council building era and were contained in the Labour government's 1965 National Plan, which proposed to increase the

annual rate of new house completions to 500 000 by 1970. The number of 'utopian' system-built dwellings within this total was intended to rise from 38 000 in 1965 to 100 000 in 1970.

But like previous housing targets, those of the National Plan were destined not to be realised. For while the output of housing, divided equally between public and private sectors, steadily rose until it almost reached 500 000 annual completions, a radical transformation in the economic role of the house itself was already beginning to take place.

Many landlords had hung on to their properties until the return of the Conservative Party to power in 1951 in the hope that rent controls would be removed. When this failed to come about they began to sell *en masse*. Between 1951 and 1984 the number of privately rented homes was to fall from 7.5 million to 2.5 million, while the number of owner-occupied homes rose from 4 million to 13.5 million.

By 1960 it was clear to both major political parties that the rental sector

The essence of the much-criticised 'utopian' Modern housing of the postwar years. Park Hill estate in Sheffield was one of the most ambitious schemes ever completed

Attempts to humanise
such monsters, as with
the addition of a
pediment to this precast
concrete maisonette at
Thamesmead, marked
the beginning of the
DIY revolution

was set in decline. In 1963 Schedule A taxation on the imputed rental value
of owner-occupied property was abolished and this measure, coupled with
mortgage interest tax relief, confirmed the advantages of private ownership.
For a time council tenancy at subsidised rents kept pace with the growth of
the private housing market, but increasing emphasis on slum clearance and
high-density construction, coupled with the experimental and unorthodox
nature of some of the new architect-designed public sector enclaves, pushed
in a different direction from that understood by the people who were to live
in the dwellings.

The influence of the housing 'experts' was destined to re-emerge only in
the longer term, when their hands had already been prised from the controls
of housing policy. They had not only revolutionised the production of houses
by introducing machine methods, but demonstrated the feasibility of radical
new house plans to many thousands of householders. Their answer to the
problem of tiny dwellings with big space demands had been quite different

from the multiplicity of tiny mono-functional rooms favoured by the private builders of the past.

Modern architects were convinced that traditional house forms had been vitiated by new materials and methods. They were also influenced by important fresh evidence of a growing increase in the rate of new household formation and a steady reduction in family size. So they had introduced concepts like 'open planning' and 'multi-functional space' to local authority housing. On their drawing boards old-fashioned 'parlours' and 'sitting rooms' had collapsed into amorphous 'living areas'. 'Kitchens' had been enlarged to become 'kitchen diners' while 'dining rooms' shrank into 'dining alcoves' and eventually disappeared altogether. In the same way 'bedrooms' became 'study bedrooms' and new types of multi-purpose room called 'family room', 'studio', 'lounge' and 'den' made their appearance. By the mid 1960s, the most advanced public housing had abandoned traditional cellular living in favour of open-plan designs. In the very last utopian council estates like Alexandra Road and Branch Hill in Camden, tenants learned to live in dwellings where space was continuous, and inside space mingled with outside space through the agency of giant picture windows and sliding glass doors.

Although nowadays universally regarded as a failure, the era of 'expert' housing design left behind it a valuable legacy of free-thinking on the subject of interior space. The 'experts' had showed convincingly how the traditional house could be reconceived as a kind of accommodation machine. Their new 'multi-functional living space' had been devised as a planning solution for necessarily small and pinched accommodation: a solution that could create the illusion of larger spaces by dissolving the separate function of rooms.

In the event, it was left to the home owners of the 1970s and 1980s to develop this new kind of living environment, for they were the ones who made financial as well as functional sense out of it by combining it with traditional marketability. A poignant illustration of this process—and perhaps an appropriate epitaph to the era of 'utopian' housing—is the photograph reproduced here. It was taken in 1972 at Thamesmead, an architect-designed satellite town for 60 000 people developed on reclaimed marshland at Erith. It shows a precast concrete maisonette to which the tenant had added a delicate little pediment made of thin strips of wood in a desperate bid to give the industrialised dwelling something of the appearance of a Georgian house.

The coming of the knockers-through

The first economic sign of the new importance of home ownership was the notable increase in the value of owner-occupied property that accompanied the 1970s waning of the 1960s public housing programmes. Improvement grants (instituted by a Labour government as a reluctant measure to help small landlords) played a part in this, for their unforseen use to finance the upgrading and subdivision of older rental properties for sale to owner-occupiers soon consumed more money than the entire national subsidy for council rents. At the same time, the first sales of council houses by Conservative local authorities began to threaten inroads into Labour's painfully accumulated 4.5 million loyal council tenant voters. With the removal of credit controls by the incoming Conservative administration in 1970, these pressures combined to drive up demand for owner-occupied housing and prices began to rise rapidly. In August 1971 a Nationwide Building Society report had showed that average house prices had risen by £100 per month during the first six months of the year, a rate of increase greater than that experienced in the whole of 1970. This was the steepening end of a graph of rising values that, virtually unnoticed, had already pushed prices up 48 per cent since 1966. In the prosperous South-East of England the increase was even more pronounced at 59 per cent.

Thus began the great bull market in housing that, apart from minor fluctuations, was not to end for 20 years. From the late 1960s until the late 1980s house prices withstood every vagary of the economy and steadily increased year on year. Great economic crises like the Arab oil embargo, the miners' strike and the Three-day Week had scarcely any more effect than the fall of the Conservative government in 1974, the Winter of Discontent, the 1981 recession or the Falklands War. Throughout this period new construction consistently lagged behind demand, but finance for mortgages was never lacking. With money supply virtually uncontrolled, higher mortgage interest rates, accompanied by higher rates to investors, brought more and more money into the building societies for lending to homeowners. In 1957 only five per cent of the nation's savings had been held by the building societies, as against 16 per cent invested in the stock market. By 1974, the building societies had doubled their share of the nation's savings at the expense of the stock market and average house prices had doubled, from £5000 in

1970 to £10500. By 1983 the Stock Exchange itself was predicting the extinction of the private investor by the year 2000 while the building societies looked forward to total assets of £1 trillion and annual advances of £90 billion in the same year.

In the event, house prices stayed ahead of inflation throughout the troubled economy of the 1970s and only paused briefly during the recession of 1981 at average levels three times higher than those of 1974. By the end of 1987, when the housing market finally did run out of steam, the price of the average house stood at nearly £50 000.

Bald figures like this cannot bring to life the full experience of the housing counter-revolution that accompanied the fall of the public sector; a counter-revolution that affected virtually every household in the land. The 1960s was the first decade for 50 years in which too much money had been able to chase too few houses. The consequences were both good and bad. One of the earliest developments was the focus of attention on older dwellings in the inner cities, where neglect had ravaged once-elegant squares and avenues. Thanks to government grants and middle-class determination, these areas, originally slated for demolition and redevelopment, now took on a new lease of life and began to claw their way back into respectability. Spared certain death by bulldozer, thousands of large London houses became the scene of battles between tenants and owners that ended with the virtual extinction of the last remnants of rent-controlled tenancy in places like Islington, Stockwell, Fulham and Putney. This is also true of their equivalents in large provincial cities.

A keen observer of the first 'battle of the tenures' that took place in the London Borough of Islington in the 1960s was Michael Thompson, then an economics student and part-time building worker, who subsequently wrote about his experiences in his book *Rubbish Theory*.[1] Thompson identified his 1960s combatants as middle class 'knockers-through' who were gradually ousting working-class sitting tenants with names like 'Ron and Cliff' and thus 'gentrifying' the borough. He analysed their opposing home improvement strategies as follows:

The Knocker-Through makes his early Victorian house older by fitting a six-panelled Georgian front door with exact reproduction brass door furniture from Beardmore's and painting it either a classic dull colour such as Adam Gold or Thames Green or, better still, black or white. His 'Ron-and-Cliff' neighbour makes his house younger by flushing the original four-panelled door with hardboard, fitting pressed steel or brushed aluminium door furniture such as one would find on a modern private estate and in the local hardware shop, and painting it in a contemporary bright colour such as Canary Yellow or Capri Blue. The

The vast areas of semi-detached housing built prior to World War Two, like this Watford suburb, were the first to undergo DIY reconstruction

'Knocker-Through' ... is trying ... to push his house from the rubbish to the durable category. His neighbour, living in a world of transience, is trying, rather unsuccessfully, to prevent his house from sliding further down the slippery slope from the transient to the rubbish category.

During the 1960s, when all this was happening, there was no such thing as a 'DIY industry'. The 'knockers-through' had to make do with hired itinerant building labour, their own amateur efforts and building materials and components bought from trade suppliers. What they achieved with these ingredients seemed more remarkable then than it does now, for a corollary of the centuries-long primacy of rental had been the landlord's responsibility for repairs and maintenance. At that time ordinary people were simply not attuned to the idea of carrying out building work themselves. Even plumbing, today an almost completely consumerised industry with all its components redesigned and labelled for amateur installers, was then an arcane trade protected by its own terminology of lead, tallow, tampins, bobbins, smudge and mandrels. But the 'knockers-through' were not deterred by these complexities. As time passed, Thompson witnessed their at-first isolated and then universal successes. This is his description of an early triumph of gentrification in Islington:

> Here in the middle of all these uniformly dilapidated houses is one, immaculately painted, Thames Green with orange front door complete with six fielded panels, brass dolphin knocker and huge brass letter-plate to match. The leaded fanlight has been painstakingly repaired and, affixed to brickwork at the side of the door, is a blue and white enamel number plate: a little touch of provincial France proclaiming that the owner drinks Hirondelle Vin Ordinaire with his Quiche Lorraine for his dinner and not light ale with ham-and-egg-pie for his tea. The cast iron balconies to the first floor windows are gay with geraniums and painted shiny black. Likewise the front railing, through which is visible, thanks to the enormously enlarged basement window (which has, not closed white net curtains, but a fully retracted navy blue blind), the basement kitchen. Directly under the window is a two-bowl twin-drainer stainless steel sink with mixer taps and waste disposal unit. On each side it is flanked by formica-topped Wrighton units and the walls are clad with similar cupboards and clear polyurethane-sealed knotty pine matching. We catch a glimpse of a stuffed pike in a bow-fronted glass case fixed to the chimney breast, and below this, the space left by the now obsolete fireplace opening has been cunningly utilised as a mini wine cellar and is filled by a metal and beechwood bottle-rack. The dividing wall has been knocked through, and an RSJ (Rolled Steel Joist, known in the trade as an 'Irish Jay') inserted and clad in the ubiquitous knotty pine, and so the heather-brown hexagonal quarry-tile floor extends in one unbroken sweep from the kitchen sink, through the rear dining area to the hardwood sill of the large french windows which open to the patio, paved with Staffordshire blue bricks, and the garden beyond. We cannot help but notice the pine farmhouse table from Heals, the bright red bentwood chairs from Habitat, some large gilt letters in a bold type salvaged from a Victorian grocer's shopfront, and a row of large blue jars with ground glass tops, similarly salvaged from an archaic chemists and bearing in gold lettering the abbreviated names of assorted poisons. And so I could go on: every feature, every lick of paint, once one has learned the language, a clear statement proclaiming the presence of the frontier middle class.

Like a revisionist historian of the Old West, Thompson saw both sides of the gentrification battle. He understood the inevitability of the triumph of the 'frontier middle class', but he was also conscious of the warrior nobility of the world of 'Ron-and-Cliff' to which he paid tribute:

[Their] . . . world bereft of durables is spectacularly competitive. Along with their flushed front doors go plastic flowers, nylon net curtains, highly polished motors, and the whole well-scrubbed, sharply-dressed, cigar smoking, fiver-waving, round-buyer bravado of the Saturday night 'dahn the boozer'. The whole business of 'putting on the style'—the devotion to sport, often expensive sports like power-boat racing, duck-shooting, or trout or shark-fishing; the gambling; the leather coats, Silver-Cross prams and elaborate hair-dos of their wives; the conspicuous consumption of drink, tobacco, sea-foods, and mohair suitings beloved by street traders, crash-repair specialists, offset lithographers, asphalters, and self-employed central-heating engineers, carpenters and ornamental plasterers—all serves to define an aristocracy of transience, piratically scornful of those who put their trust in durables, and viciously exclusive of social rubbish. Their motto is 'easy come easy go', for in the Land of Transience, the man with the highest turnover rules, OK? The Ron-and-Cliff man (is like) the Bedouin. 'All his values are those of a warrior society, in which the two dominant themes are courage and generosity. By displaying courage in war and so obtaining plunder he gains his livelihood. Through generosity he disposes of what he owns. To be mean implies a want of confidence in one's ability to gain more plunder.'

Thompson's opinion was that the triumph of the 'knockers-through' came from their capacity to 'make things durable'. A power that grew in turn from their 'control over knowledge'—in their case knowledge of the housing market—a knowledge that only the middle classes possessed. By the time this knowledge was generalised—that is, by the time 'Ron-and-Cliff' heard about it—it was bound to be too late for them to climb aboard. They would never be as well-placed again as they had been in those far-off days when they were rent-controlled tenants occupying vast run-down houses in Islington.

What Thompson could not have foreseen at the time he wrote was that the 'durables value' the 'knockers-through' strove to create had nothing to do with permanence. Instead it was no more than a counter in another game of transience: the transience of the emerging professional owner-occupier who sooner or later 'cashed-out' of his or her Islington dwelling and moved on to ride the house-price escalator somewhere else. The 'owner-speculators' satirised in this newspaper article of 1976 contrast bleakly with the earnest 'knockers-through' of only a few years before:

Keep moving. Keep moving up. Don't worry about a big mortgage. Get a long

mortgage with the lowest payments available, because you'll never pay
it off anyway.

Never, never rent. That is the same as sitting still, gaining no equity, and
prices will be moving up, just beyond reach.

Spend every penny you can get your hands on. If you get a Christmas bonus
put in a swimming pool. If you lose your job, take your redundancy money and
put in a new kitchen.

Don't think of your house as a home. Think of it as an investment.

Forget sentiment. Don't put down roots. If your children complain that they're
always at a new school, ignore them.

The main thing is to get started. Five years from now, the same estate agent
will shake his head sadly, and say he has nothing available for less than £100000.

Adept at trading up, and hardened to exploiting 'durable values', it was
these new-style homeowners who took over the genteel market created by
the 'knockers-through' and parlayed it into the greatest housing boom of all.
One that was only to end in paralysis late in the 1980s. By that time the total
value of all the owner-occupied housing stock in the country had risen
twenty-fold, from £50 billion in 1968 to a staggering £1000 billion—the
largest concentration of capital in the nation.

Financing the domestic revolution

It was in the 1970s that mortgage lending turned into a means of financing home improvements. For centuries the term 'mortgage' meant a loan secured against the value of a house, generally to be repaid over ten to 20 years; then suddenly it became a form of short-term 'bridging finance'. As the 1970s turned into 1980s the progressive alienation of mortgage finance from new construction that this change brought about became dramatically obvious. In 1965 just over 200000 new private houses were built, but the building societies made 382000 loans on houses totalling £800 million. In 1972 new house construction had fallen to 190000 private dwellings but 681000 loans on houses were made with a total value of £3600 million. By 1976 a total of 715000 loans on houses worth £6100 million accompanied a bare 170000 new house completions. By 1986, such was the growth of the 'revolving door' mortgage market in the last phase of the housing boom, that the number of loans on houses had doubled to 1500000 with a value of £32000 million—while new house building still dragged along at the 1972 level.

What these statistics reveal is the emergence of a real-market in houses for the first time, almost like a branch of the Stock Exchange. By the mid 1970s 'trading up' by moving from house to house—in 70 per cent of cases this was a move of less than 5 miles—had become largely a matter of optimised financial gain. It was for this reason that the average term of each mortgage sank to 3–5 years. The 20 years referred to in the mortgage documents possessed a merely nominal significance, indeed it soon rose to hypothetical levels such as 25 or 40 years in anticipation of frequent refinancing. Perhaps the most eloquent proof of the new immateriality of the mortgage term was contained in this advice from American property commentator Robert Bruss quoted in an English newspaper in 1976: 'At age 70 you should have no trouble getting a 25-year mortgage. My parents (ages 84 and 75) got a 30-year mortgage with only a 10 per cent down payment.'

Another aspect of the new housing market took the form of a revised pattern of institutional lending, this time designed to enable homeowners to get their hands on the increasing cash value of their 'investments-for-living-in' without the inconvenience of having to sell them. This process, straddling the grey area between 'top-up' loans to householders made over the term of their existing mortgage and 'personal loans' secured on property, soon earned the soubriquet 'equity leakage'—meaning the use of a mortgage advance for any purposes other than buying a house.

As early as 1970, 'top-up loans amounted to 13 per cent of all building society lending, and even then they were beginning to attract attention. In 1971 a government committee on consumer credit chaired by Lord Crowther reported:

> While a loan on first mortgage for the purchase of a house for occupation is not a matter on which we have much to say, the borrowing of money on a house already owned and the use of the money for consumption purposes may bring the transaction into the very centre of our proper concern. Indeed ... the offering of loans for consumption purposes secured on second mortgage is a recent development that raises a number of questions.

These questions were to remain unanswered for a number of years, even though equity leakage loans were increasingly being openly offered. As early

(LEFT) The banks led the way in making the connection between credit and home improvements. A Barclaycard advertisement, 1971. (RIGHT) A 1971 Lloyds Bank advertisement making a direct connection between marriage, home improvements, prosperity and credit. (ABOVE) At the height of the boom, advertising for loans secured against the soaring value of houses appeared daily in every newspaper. This example is from the *London Standard*, 19th March, 1986

as 1972, this advertisement for the finance company United Dominions Trust frequently appeared in the popular press:

Cash in on the increasing value of your home without selling it. How much do you owe on your mortgage? Now how does it compare with the present value of your home? The difference could mean a very useful source of credit.

At that time, with total mortgage advances limited to about £2700 million a year, the leakage of housing credit into general consumption was estimated to be of the order of two or three per cent. But with the passage of time it began to grow as fast as the housing market itself. By the mid 1980s, the building societies were lending £1000 million every week and advertisements for equity loans appeared regularly on the front page solus spot of every daily newspaper. A typical advertisement from this later period reads:

Unlock your capital by unlocking your mortgage. Release thousands of £££'s profit in your house today enabling you to: put money in the bank, reduce your outgoings, improve your home, pay off expensive loans and overdrafts ...

The growth of mortgage finance had been so spectacular, and the parallel decline of manufacturing industry so pronounced, that by 1985 anomalous situations had arisen. The second mortgage market alone was worth more than the British motor industry. In March 1985 the Bank of England issued a warning to the clearing banks about the economic consequences of equity leakage from mortgage finance and produced figures showing that it had increased from £1500 million in 1979 to £7200 million in 1984. Up from three per cent to 30 per cent.

But by then the most obvious of the questions raised by Lord Crowther could be answered. Notwithstanding much wild talk of balance-of-payments-ruining imported kitchens, foreign cars and foreign holidays, it appeared from the rapid growth of the home improvement industry that most equity leakage was being used to pay for home improvements. Thus the modern Do-It-Yourself industry with its 'big shed' architecture and suburban shopping locations was founded upon mortgage money that had 'leaked out' into consumption. By 1985, with a turnover of £7 billion, the home improvement industry had come of age. By 1988, the year the housing market finally stalled, one eighth of the building materials, components and construction plant sold in Britain went across the counters of more than 2500 new DIY stores to amateur home-improvers beavering away on home extensions, loft conversions and fitted kitchens.

From the very beginning, what homeowners might actually do with the extra money they borrowed on the security of their houses had been suggested to them by the lenders themselves, led by the building societies, banks and finance houses that already advertised heavily to homeowners. Barclaycard was early in the field with an advertisement showing a house furnished and carpeted with credit cards. Lloyd's Bank arrayed a full complement of consumer durables, including a speedboat and a caravan, alongside a smiling bride in nuptial gown on the front lawn of a suburban house. By 1985, an indication of the burgeoning ambitions of equity leakers could be gauged from a Bristol and West building society advertisement showing a young couple, a new car and a yacht in front of the Taj Mahal.

Throughout the housing boom years, borrowing against equity operated as a kind of turbocharger for the housing market. Credit created by increasing prices was used by 'traders-up' and 'stay-putters' alike to pay for a galaxy of housing extras that helped increase the value of their homes and thus gave a power boost to the whole house-price economy. But this macroeconomic effect was not its microeconomic purpose. Underlying the massive growth in housing credit and the birth and spectacular growth of the DIY industry was a huge new technological input into suburban life that affected every household in the land.

Thousands of small terraced pre-1914 houses and many of the postwar houses of the 1940s, 1950s and 1960s had been built with tiny rooms and even tinier kitchens. They were simply not large enough to receive the flood of new consumer durables that increasingly defined an acceptable standard of living as the wars and disasters of the first half of the century faded into the past. A typical case was the Harold Hill council estate near Romford, in Essex. Begun in 1947 as London overspill housing for bombed-out East End families, it was finished 20 years later, just as the sale of council houses began. So significant in political terms was this step seen to be that Margaret Thatcher, then housing minister in the Conservative government led by Edward Heath, herself handed over the keys to the first Harold Hill purchaser in 1971. The next 20 years was to see the sale of almost all the houses on the estate and a massive programme of home improvements that led to a number of them actually doubling in size.

Harold Hill is a perfect example of the operations of the DIY economy during the boom housing years and the Martin Pover photographs in these pages of the houses, their occupants and the transformations that they wrought, give an unrivalled impression of a process that was repeated in millions of houses all over the country.

Between 1951 and 1984, the proportion of households in Britain without a fixed bath fell from 40 per cent to two per cent. The number of television sets in houses rose from 2000 to 15 million, the number of cars from three million to 17 million, the number of refrigerators from three million to 21 million, the number of freezers from 400 000 to 12 million—and so on through the entire ever-expanding range of consumer durables. Although accurate figures have not been compiled, it is safe to say that the bulk of the huge task of enlargement, adaptation and installation that was necessary to accommodate this unprecedented bonanza was carried out by householders themselves, as at Harold Hill.

The whole phenomenon had a kind of inevitability about it. It was as though the moment the massive production of houses stopped, the production of consumer goods like refrigerators, washers, TVs and cars increased to fill the vacuum. And soon it appeared that a wonderfully symbiotic relationship had developed between these two poles of the consumer lifestyle. The houses that increased in value through scarcity were used as collateral to buy the consumer goods that increased in profusion. And the real miracle was that house prices increased so much that they not only produced sufficient credit to buy all these consumer durables; they provided enough purchasing power to found a whole retail support industry to solve the space problem posed by the inadequate size of the houses into which they had to fit.

It was here that the theories of 'open planning' and 'multi-functional space'

Frank and Reta Coffin's house at Harold Hill, Essex. Unique in being virtually unaltered 45 years after it was built as a council house

Mrs Reta Coffin in her sitting room at Harold Hill. The interior of the house too retains its original division into separate rooms

Mr and Mrs Richards in the enlarged multifunctional living area created by home improvements

Amersham Road, Harold Hill. A perfect example of a postwar suburb 'tuned up' by DIY with the aid of housing boom money

Mr and Mrs Wright's house in North Hill Drive, Harold Hill. Note the addition of an assertive precast concrete honeycomb garden wall

Mr and Mrs Wright in their living area, greatly enlarged from the original separate rooms by DIY alterations and extensions

Number 49 Gooshay's Drive, Harold Hill. A tasteful DIY refronting of a former council house embodying elements of the traditional Essex wood vernacular

The interior of 49 Gooshay's Drive, where swooping arches reveal the disappearance of partition walls in the pursuit of space within a tiny dwelling

(ABOVE) Motors are important icons in suburban life. Two young men in a smart Cortina, Straight Road, Harold Hill, 1991. Front doors at Harold Hill tell the story of DIY. The 'original equipment' door (OPPOSITE LEFT) is now a rarity. More common is an 'ultimate porch extension' (OPPOSITE RIGHT).

(LEFT) All the elements of the consumer lifestyle in Straight Road, Harold Hill. Remodelled houses with front gardens full of up-market vehicles.

taught by the postwar housing experts came into their own again. The English middle classes had held out against domestic informality for a whole generation after the war. At first they hid their television sets inside antique armoires and their hi-fi speakers behind panelling. But it didn't last for long. In the end it was television that broke down the remaining barriers of cellular formality. People who did not give in to 'multi-functional space' were compelled either to bolt their meals so as not to miss their favourite programmes, balance trays on their laps in front of the TV or eat at the kitchen table with a TV in the kitchen—cooking and watching, watching and cooking. Soon every pretence collapsed and multi-functional space invaded every class of dwelling. In vast numbers of households cooking was more or less abandoned in favour of TV dinners, precooked food or 'grazing'—endless snacking instead of mealtimes. Throughout the suburbs DIY, TV and informality ruled.

The possibility of accommodating all this may have been demonstrated two decades earlier by the housing experts of the 'modern' era, but the new owner-speculators of the housing boom rejected the square, bald interiors that

175 · THE ELECTRONIC COTTAGE

the experts had given to their own utopian designs. Instead they cunningly combined the functional space-utilisation of 'modern' architecture with the old image-appeal of the housing resale market. What they wanted were new big houses that looked like old small houses, and the means to achieve this lay to hand in their own burgeoning DIY industry.

Through loan finance, the mass-marketing of the house as a 'consumer

envelope'—as opposed to the social service 'unit of accommodation' dreamed of by postwar socialist politicians—finally became a reality. For a time the ordinary house became a unique microeconomic sinking fund that financed its own enlargement and improvement. With the coming of age of DIY, the economic circle was complete.

(ABOVE) The twilight of English formality. Father
cuts the roast at a family Sunday lunch in 1938.
Takeaways and eating in bed were unknown

(ABOVE RIGHT) The rise of American informality.
This American family, also photographed in 1938,
is restrained by modern standards of relaxation.
But the children sprawling on the floor
foreshadow the behavioural consequences of
the wartime American invasion

The DIY Cathedral

The building is huge and square, with dull blue profiled steel-sheet cladding and bits of brickwork round its rows of glass doors. It is built in the middle of a vast carpark with gleaming trolleys lined up like rolling stock alongside the cars. Unisex couples in jeans, tee-shirts and trainers are levering pre-painted windows, bags of cement, lawn furniture, wood burning stoves and Grecian urns ('Great value at £1.99') onto roof racks and into hatchbacks or battered estate cars that have seen better days. It is Texas Homecare on a summer weekend in the mid 1980s, at the height of the housing boom. The store is open late. Inside, the clack-clack of the credit card machines almost drowns the background music and the occasional urgent announcements over the public address system: 'Mr Preston or Mr Toy to the House of Heating please ... Mr Preston or Mr Toy to the House of Heating please ...'

In the 1980s, DIY was the temple of homeowners equity, the bring-and-buy bargain basement of the housing market. The Labour politicians who, throughout the decade, regularly announced that it would cost £7 billion or £10 billion or £20 billion to shore up postwar council housing, hospitals, schools and all the rest of the crumbling public estate never took a serious look at DIY. But that was where the real money was. By the mid 1980s, enough borrowed and after-tax money to do everything they wanted was chasing the elusive goal of home improvement through its cavernous big sheds. By the time the housing bubble burst the annual figure spent on DIY had risen to an estimated £9 billion: nine times the development cost of Concorde, twice the annual earnings of tourism and as much as an entire year's earnings from North Sea oil. According to market analysts Mintel, nearly ten per cent of all building materials were being sold retail—that is, through DIY stores—by 1984. By 1987 this proportion was up to 15 per cent. All of it consumerised into easy-carry ten kilogram bags of premixed cement and sand, short lengths of timber with a price sticker on every one, and shrink-wrapped plumbing fittings with instructions attached.

In 1986 more than one million homeowners extended their homes upwards, downwards or sideways, spending an average of £4000 per household. Nearly half of them installed new kitchens, a fifth put on a porch and another fifth added a new bathroom or a new lavatory. Only loft conversions and prefabricated garages racked up a lower output than the year before. But, as Mintel advised: 'The prospect of extension work on the one million council houses that have been sold into the private sector since 1980 gives all suppliers grounds for optimism'.

They are certainly optimistic at our Texas superstore. Inside the cavernous, windowless steel-frame emporium there is the Dolby hush of a great cathedral. The walls are concrete block, painted blue with supergraphic stripes that engulf all projections like the tide-mark in the temple of Abu Simbel. The whole of one end is given over to what looks like a real two-storey house shoehorned so tightly into the mighty space that its chimney pots graze the roof cladding far above. But it is not so much a real house as a surreal house. Its walls are plastic brick-lookalike panels, its bow windows with their random bulls-eye lights will never feel a spot of rain. The plan of the house is literally fantastic. Every room on the ground floor is a demonstration kitchen. There is the Panorama (light brown), the Astral (green), the Cordoba (dark brown), the Geneva (cream), the Vogue (double Jersey cream) and the Apex, which is in white. No real cooking ever takes place in these kitchens because all the implements are concealed but at £976.99 a throw, who's complaining? On the first floor of the house every room is a bedroom with an *en-suite* bathroom, seven in all. In one of them is the incongruous notice 'Shopthieves will be prosecuted.' Who are the 'shopthieves' and what would they steal? Surely not the Anderson Regency fire surround with its little Corinthian columns and swags, light as a feather—and small enough for the tiniest starter-home. Perhaps the large glazed and framed print of plough horses on a cliff over the sea at £49.99? Or the nest of Regency tables, small but perfectly formed, for £39.99. Everything in this world of DIY looks ordinary at first, but then strange. Why is there a 'cracked ice' pattern on the stick-on ceiling tiles? Why are the huge 94-litre plastic dustbins wafer-thin, even though they look as strong as galvanised steel industrial paladins? And the fast-selling Grecian urns that are everywhere; they would just about pass muster long-shot in a biblical drama, but when you pick one up it is so light that the wind would blow it right off the patio into the plastic-lined fishpond.

Collected together like this all the elements of DIY seem an illusion. The small children who accompany their parents around the store keep on mistaking it for a giant toy shop: one boy runs to a hopper full of orange plastic ball-cock floats and bounces one across the aisle. His mother explains patiently that it is not a ball but a building element, part of a multi-billion pound industry. But then the parents too are in a daze, muttering quietly to one another about the relative merits of patterns and designs when really they are concentrating on the super-prominent price tickets in ninety-nines.

Vast DIY stores like his Homebase provided everything for the DIY transformation of the home, even inviting house names

£999.99 for a full gas central heating system; £79.99 for a real stone hearth; £19.99 for lengths of plastic guttering and just 99p for a bag of charcoal barbecue fuel 'made in Spain'.

The implications of this atomised menagerie of construction bits and pieces are breathtaking. Plumbing, that noble trade whose 24-hour visiting cards litter the streets of London, is hereby reduced to a mountain of shrink-wrapped, bar-coded fittings and individually-priced lengths of plastic pipe. Anyone can do it now. The instructions are stapled to the bag, showing encouraging pictures of pretty girls installing sinks without even breaking their nails. Nor is DIY confined to small stuff like this. A 1985 survey showed that a significant proportion of the sales of heavy plant—small dump trucks, cement mixers, power tools, pallets of concrete blocks, sand and ballast, floor joists, roof trusses, reinforcing bars, steel beams, double garage doors and swimming pool kits—all tottered away in, on or behind cars, vans and pick-up trucks, turning Everyman into Builderman.

Consumerisation is a process whose end is easier to grasp than its means. Its end is the disappearance of a specialist skill such as painting and decorating. In the old tenancy days before homeownership and DIY, painting and decorating used to be done by reflective men of mature years who wore white coats and carried ladders and cans of paint. Now it is a game played by young marrieds when they move into their new home with their dog. The more paint they can splash around before they have to go off to the cash dispenser, the more fun it is.

A consumerised trade is one that is dominated by punters not practitioners. In the world of construction, carpentry and joinery used to be expert activities that required special tools and considerable training. In recognition of this, large quantities of sawn or planed timber used to be bought wholesale and stored in the open at builders' yards. Now the really large stocks of wood are found inside retail DIY stores with a separate price ticket on every length. At the same time, real carpenters and joiners have become virtually extinct and, although everybody has a complete set of power woodworking tools out of the Argos catalogue, nobody knows how to fit pieces of wood together without glue any more.

The first response of the building trade to consumerisation was to blame it all on 'cowboys'. Cowboys were 'romantic' figures, irresponsible vaga-bonds who came from nowhere, three to a pick-up truck, took advance payments from little old ladies and were never seen again. Either that, or they started repairing the roof and then went off to live in Spain about Christmas time. The industry made numerous straight-faced attempts to get cowboys outlawed. But real builders are only superficially hard nuts. Like the government and the police force, they have a pathetic faith in certificates, institutes, licences, contracts, guarantees and insurance of all kinds.

The real problem with the battle against the cowboys in the building trade was the classic one of not recognising the real enemy. It was no good lecturing the average householder on the dangers of hiring an unqualified, uncertified, uninsured loft conversion expert when you were looking one straight in the eyes. 'We have seen the enemy and he is us' should have been the householders' motto. Despite the fine performance put on by concerned and indignant industry representatives, it was self-evident that the real cowboys in the housing industry were not the non-VAT-paying fly-by-night bandits of popular fiction but ordinary people convinced by DIY commercials on television that they could do anything they wanted to in the building line on their own.

The anti-cowboy lobbyists in the housebuilding industry never dared face this awful truth. It was DIY that threatened them, not cowboys. The cowboys were imaginary. They were not just up against a few hooligans. They were up against a £6 billion a year industry with a TV-reinforced grip on virtually every home in the country, a supply system with the freedom of the motorway network, a complex of vast distribution centres and direct access to bulk-purchased imported building materials. For years the charade went on and on, the anti-cowboy lobby punching into the air, the DIY family piling more and more building materials and equipment onto their roof-racks and carrying it home.

All that was before the recession. Now things are different. With the passing of the bull housing market for the first time in a generation, the phantom cowboys have vanished over the horizon, barely even pausing to run their pick-up trucks through an auction or wave their hats in the air.

And what will happen to the real cowboys, the seasoned DIYers of the suburbs? For years they cheerfully paid through the nose for everything. They bought nails and screws in penny packets, plumbing fittings individually wrapped, timber that nobody else would use and tools that broke first-go. They always paid top whack for everything and couldn't even reclaim the VAT. Of course whatever they spent was offset by tax-free capital gains on the houses they worked on that at least equalled their annual earnings. But now that is over. If the real construction industry is already calling in the receiver, laying-off labour and bidding below cost just to maintain cash flow, what chance does the amateur cowboy have now?

Actually, it's a better one than you might think. Two years after the housing market went into a coma, there is still reckoned to be about £750 billion of untapped equity in the 14 million owner occupied homes of the UK. That is equal to two years of consumer spending, even without the belt-tightening that low retail sales indicate has actually taken place.

Today the economic, social and employment ramifications of the mortgage market are so enormous that its future is a political question, not simply a matter to be settled by market forces. In effect neither major party can allow house prices to collapse—as opposed to stagnate—however grave the consequences for other sectors of the economy. This means that the massive equity tied up in homeownership is more than ever under the control of consumers and not the government, the banks or the building societies. Whatever its long term consequences may be, it is a fact that ever since homeowner's equity began building in the late 1960s the power of government over housing has steadily diminished.

The electronic cottage

Next time you drive through an English suburb you should look carefully at the houses that you pass. In nearly every case they are not as they were originally built, but have undergone considerable changes. Nearly all will actually be larger because an extension of one sort or another has been added, often on more than one floor beneath the same roofline so that the join is virtually invisible. Most will have replacement windows with their original softwood or galvanised frames replaced by double glazing in uPVC or aluminium. Many will have a new front door incorporating a half-round fanlight. Often the whole of what was once a front garden, conceived when owning one car was unusual and multiple car ownership was a business only for Hollywood film stars, will have been paved or gravelled over to make room for these ubiquitous vehicles. In a few cases there will even be a splendid after-market portico outside the front door, supported by glass fibre-reinforced plastic columns.

These are the external signs of change, but they are as nothing compared to what has been done internally to these houses. Like the Six Million Dollar Man, they look normal on the outside but inside they are more than half robotised. Scarcely one in a hundred of these houses has not been 'knocked through' so that its front and back living rooms are joined into one large space by the agency of a wooden or steel joist, where the dividing wall used to be. Perhaps one in a thousand has not had central heating installed, along with a second bathroom, a new kitchen (or two or three) as fashions have changed. Successive owners, each more ambitious than the last, have transformed these houses. First they removed the partition walls that once separated the small formal rooms to create larger spaces and then they enlarged these spaces by adding conservatories, sun rooms, granny flats, loft conversions, spiral wine cellars, bedrooms over the garage, pools in the garden (even where there appears to be insufficient room) and a new carport with hardstanding to park a caravan or store a boat during the winter.

There are other important differences between the way the facelifted suburban houses of the present look and their original appearance but they are not conspicuous ones. So common has the sight become that one no longer notices a TV aerial on a chimney, or the dish of a satellite receiver angled at 28 degrees on a south-facing wall. But even microwave and satellite dishes are prominent compared to the other domestic indicators of the massive energy and information technology transformations that have taken place within our houses. Unlike any previous houses in history, all twentieth century dwellings whatever their actual physical age can receive electronic information from all over the world in sounds and pictures. In fact the quantity and variety of the image, sound and information technology that is packed into the smallest suburban house today would amaze a visitor from a mere half-century ago.

Virtually without exception, all our houses are connected by unseen cables to a perpetual electric power supply. More wires connect our telephones by landline, microwave link and satellite to virtually all the other houses in the world. Then there are the slave devices that live off these invisible sources of power and information. There are machines that repeat and record messages when no one is at home, and time-clocks that switch on lights, record television programmes and cook dinners without human intervention. There are disc and tape players, television sets in several rooms, perhaps a couple of micro computers and cordless telephones. There are sound systems and video systems wired into the house as deeply as if they were parts of its nervous system. There are racks of compact discs and audio cassettes, piles of video tapes and stacks of old albums hidden away in cupboards. There are speakers ranging from flimsy Walkman headphones to suspended boxes as large as antique chests. Everywhere there are electric motors driving water pumps, agitators, compressors, timers, vacuum cleaners, fans, dehumidifiers, turn-tables, hard and floppy disk drives, daisy-wheel printers, dot-matrix printers, laser and bubble-jet printers, digital clocks and radio-controlled model cars and boats. In the kitchen there is a freezer that will keep food fresh forever, a refrigerator that defrosts itself when necessary and makes ice cubes all the time. There is a food-processor, a microwave with a timer, an oven that comes on and goes off by itself. A washing machine and a dishwasher are plumbed into the pipes that bring clean water into the heart of the house and feed into the drains that carry dirty water away. These two machines alone whirr and slosh through preplanned cycles day after day like galley slaves.

Although on average fewer than three people live in each of these houses, between them they have more personal possessions than a typical Victorian family of six would have believed possible. They have walk-in cupboards and wardrobes full of clothes—and an astonishing amount of furniture besides. There are sideboards, dining tables, three-piece suites, occasional tables, reclining chairs, shelves and racks, dressing tables, padded bed-heads and decorated mantelpieces. There are old-looking fire irons, burnished copper kettles, horse brasses and warming pans. There are small statues, paintings, prints, photographs, posters, figurines, books, plates, bronzes, vases, flowers, embroidery, mementoes, plaques, cups and glasses of every imaginable sort. Nor does the cornucopia of possessions stop at the door of the house. Outside are the cars—mobile satellites of the home that are used like giant briefcases or holdalls, adept also at towing trailers with bikes, boats, waterskis, camping gear or even caravans. They boast engines of enormous power and subsystems of great complexity. Beneath their sleek metal skins lie fuel tanks filled with petroleum extracted from the bowels of the earth or drawn from the bottom of the sea. Under their bonnets are 16-valve engines with computerised ignition systems and automated heating, ventilating and cooling systems that work better than those in the house itself. There are other subsystems almost too numerous to list here: wiper motors, washer motors, window motors, rear view mirror motors and seat adjustment motors, thermostats and thermometers that emit an audible warning when the temperature drops below freezing, speedometers that sound an alarm when the car exceeds the legal speed limit . . .

Very little of this miraculous inventory of indoor and outdoor equipment existed when most of these houses were built. Certainly none of it was freely available or destined to be grasped by the hands of ordinary people. It is all of recent invention and manufacture. Even the apparently antique items are most likely to be modern reproductions. The idea of the new-looking-old is printed right through the house and its contents. Indeed, its very construction embodies a thousand examples of this paradox with fake leaded lights and bull's eye windows, the lack of a chimney (because central heating has replaced the open fire) but a fake fireplace is present nevertheless, a front door fanlight set into the door itself, not mounted above it (because the ceiling inside is too low). All of these period solecisms show us that, while the exact imitation of history is obviously not the object of the exercise, the house is intended to look old. In all probability old enough to convince an eighteenth century time traveller, who would certainly not recognise a washing machine or a video cassette recorder. Such a visitor would instantly identify a contemporary house and walk straight up to the front door. He would probably hesitate before the glass front of a modern office block and recoil in horror from the forbidding profiled-steel walls of a giant distribution centre beside a motorway.

The unique combination of traditional appearance with unhistorical substance is a very important attribute of the electronic cottage and one that is little understood. We live in a world of products formed by an unseen process of design that flows around us like electricity yet very few of our houses are 'designer objects' like an Armani suit or a Porsche car. Our electronic cottages may envelope a lifestyle that is continually updated by technology, but they themselves are identified with traditional values.

Twenty-five years ago, before the home improvement industry as we understand it today even existed, an architect named William Cowburn published an influential article on the importance of tradition in the design of speculative housing.[2] Cowburn's conclusion was that it was not so much the presence of authentic traditional details that was important to private house buyers, but the predictability of traditional house plans and elevations as well as the proportional moderation in everything from size to decoration that was the hallmark of the traditional builder. What house buyers in the 1960s required was:

> . . . a traditional detached bungalow but with rooms in the roof space with dormer windows, placed within a clearly defined plot, which should face onto an ordinary road; that is, the road and layout should imply no community grouping, and should be fairly anonymous, both in their indications of ways in and out, particularly in relation to the more central town or village areas.

Describing the ideal buyer's house, Cowburn went on:

> The detailing of the house should be extremely plain. With the windows no more than screens across holes in walls and the fascias no more than terminations to take gutters. There is little attempt to 'bend' the detailed design to achieve sculptural or spatial effects, although a degree of control over the 'boldness' of the design is exercised by the sizing of these members. There is a strong attempt to make each part 'in keeping' with the whole. There is seldom any attempt to emphasise any structural order inherent in the designs.
>
> Because he must consider resale, the pop house buyer tends to buy a universal product with a plan and layout that shows less variety than those of council houses and flats: the pop house achieves its variety through universality . . . Though this universality is in some ways inefficient, it produces a greater variety in one's way of life during one's lifespan than does a house of glove-like fit, for instance in old age where there is space for the greater number of acquisitions obtained over the years. There is a sort of classic quality engendered by the similarity of all these houses. Wherever one moves to one knows that the carpets will fit more or less and the furniture will not be out of place.

Robert Adam is another architect who has addressed this subject, writing almost a quarter of a century after Cowburn. His interest centred on the 'stealth' approach to advanced technology employed by the housebuilders of the 1980s in the construction of dwellings that look, if anything, even older-fashioned than Cowburn's 1960s 'universal product'.

In his essay 'Tin Gods and contemporary architecture',[3] Adam lists more than 30 major non-traditional materials and components that go towards creating the traditional appearance of the contemporary house. They range from concrete roof tiles and glass fibre-reinforced bituminous roofing felt, through computer-designed roof trusses, factory-produced windows and machine-made bricks, down to polymeric damp-proof courses, uPVC man-holes and drainpipes, and concrete foundations. So comprehensive is this list of advanced technology infiltrations into the housing market that it is disappointing to record that Adam himself is not impressed by it. After considering all the evidence he concludes:

> *I am absolutely appalled by the design standards of these buildings and would blanch even at the word 'architecture' being used in connection with them. But the simple truth is that they are ... very modern high-tech buildings. All their parts have been influenced by recent technological changes and they have responded to new demands from the end-user market or the construction market by improving comfort, decreasing heat-loss, lowering maintenance, easing construction by a reduction in labour, or speeding up construction by the use of prefabricated components.*

Cowburn's explanation of the preferences of home buyers before the great DIY boom began and Adam's analysis of the innovative construction of the modern house are instructive but incomplete. Neither really addresses the most important aspect of the pro-tradition anti-design prejudice of home-owners, which is that it is uniformly successful. Clearly, in 1966 as in 1990, it is householders and not housebuilders who are in charge. Whatever they want, they get and, as a result, the pervasive image of desirable housing is strongly fashion-resistant. Far from being dominated by the appearance of the newest volume-housebuilder's model, the housing market is dominated by the aggregate appearance of all its ancient predecessors. 'There is no quality' as *The Times* accurately observed in a leader in 1981 'that the public so much admires in a building as to have been standing for a very long time. And that is a quality very hard to achieve in new building'. Hard, but not impossible. Consider this advertisement for a prestigious London develop-ment:

> *These are large homes. With architectural details that long ago faded from common usage. There are upstairs verandahs, entry doors with tympanum fanlights, clerestory dormers, chamfered cornerposts, window shelves and latticed Yorkshire lights.*
>
> *The brickwork is elaborate. There are corniced chimney tops, string courses, herringbone work and ornamental flue caps. Inside the rooms flow into one another with dignity and ease. There are graceful archways, stairways with turned newels and balusters and oak handrails with volutes. There are window seats designed*

for reading by windowlight. There are fireplaces with marble hearths and wooden mantelpieces.

Naturally these houses have all of the amenities you would expect of a contemporary home of importance. But it is the details revived from long ago, from a time when architects and craftsmen worked to create homes of grace and dignity, that separate these homes from the common.

Even if we ignore the characteristic hyperbole of the writing here, it is surely remarkable that the potential for space-age automated leisure that we know to be offered by such houses should be relegated to a single sentence in the last paragraph.

Unlike the used car market, which changes and evolves as new models filter down the slippery slope of suffixes and prefixes until a 'K' registered car is no longer new but old and thus not at all fashionable, the used housing market consists of buildings more or less erected for perpetuity. The successful house of the late twentieth century is neither new nor old. It is like a car first registered in 1900 that has magically changed its prefix year after year (by this or that piece of home improvement) and so appears to be perpetually new. Perpetually—that is, a part of the ever new, product-rich but designer-resistant suburban scene that establishes the general image of successful houses everywhere.

Neither Cowburn nor Adam addressed the enormous incidence of alteration and adaptation of existing houses and the conversion of large residential and non-residential buildings into small dwellings that has taken place in the last 25 years. Cowburn, of course, wrote before this phenomenon really got under way but he would probably have taken the same view of it as Adam; that, because so much of it is unconnected with professional design, it is of limited interest to architects and designers. In this he would have been right, but also a trifle short-sighted. For in the years between his definition of what ordinary people wanted from their houses and Adam's explanation of how a later generation of high-technology builders learned to give it to them, grass-roots home improvement not only became a far bigger economic phenomenon than professional design but bigger than the housebuilding industry itself. Between 1968 and 1988 £1.75 trillion was borrowed to buy, enlarge, alter and modernise British houses. The effect was to create a fantastic explosion of possessions in space that preserved the ancient image of the house but destroyed the old culture of rooms altogether.

History may well show us that home improvement was the last craft housing industry to exist before the collapse of that fanatically-preserved traditional image and the triumph of the machine-produced single-person accommodation unit of tomorrow.

FOOTNOTES AND BIBLIOGRAPHY

CHAPTER ONE

[1]GRAHAME, K. *The wind in the willows*
Many edns., including Puffin, 1983

[2]CHANDLER, R. *The big sleep*
H. Hamilton, 1984; Penguin, 1989

[3]See [1]

[4]BRONTË, C. *Jane Eyre* Many edns.,
including Penguin, 1971

[5]TOLSTOY, L. *War and peace*
Heinemann, 1971; Pan, 1972;
Penguin, 1982; OUP, 1991

[6]BRONTË, E. *Wuthering heights*
Many edns., including Penguin,
1990

[7]AUSTEN, J. *Persuasion* Many edns.,
including Penguin 1970

[8]CHANDLER, R. *The high window*
H. Hamilton, 1984; Penguin, 1989

[9]TREMAIN, R. *Restoration*
H. Hamilton, 1989; Sceptre, 1990

[10]*Daily Mail book of house plans* Many
edns., including Plan Magazines,
1991

[11]*Daily Mail book of bungalows* Many
edns., including Associated
Newspapers, 1975. op.

[12]ORWELL, G. *1984* Many edns.,
including Penguin, 1990

[13]WILDE, O. *The portrait of Dorian Gray*
Many edns., including OUP, 1989

[14]See [6]

[15]HOGGART, R. *The uses of literacy*
Penguin, 1990

[16]AUSTEN LEIGH, E. *A memoir of Jane
Austen* Folcroft, 1979

[17]See [2]

[18]WOOLF, V. *Night and Day* Panther,
1978; Chatto, 1991

[19]MAURIER, D. du *Rebecca* Gollancz,
1980; Pan, 1976

[20]FITZGERALD, F. S. *The great Gatsby*
Many edns., including Penguin, 1990

[21]See [2]

[22]See [5]

[23]FITZGERALD, F. S. *The last tycoon*
Penguin, 1990

[24]CHRISTIE, A. *The body in the library*
Collins, 1976, 1990; Fontana, 1986

[25]WOOLF, V. *Mrs Dalloway* Panther,
1976; Chatto, 1991

[26]DICKENS, C. *Hard times* Many edns.,
including Penguin, 1990

[27]See [20]

[28]DICKENS, C. *Great expectations* Many
edns., including Penguin, 1970

CHAPTER TWO

[1]Polyclytus of Larissa, Eighth Book of
History quoted in: GRAY, C. and
GRAY, M. *The bed* Nicholson &
Watson, 1946. op.

[2]EURIPIDES 'Alcestis' in *Three plays*
trans P. Vellacott. Penguin, 1953. op.
(Penguin, 1970)

[3]CARTER, H. and MACE, A. C. *The
tomb of Tutankhamen* Cassell, 1933.
op.

[4]Phrynichus, from ATHENAEUS *The
Deipnosophists* trans C. B. Gulik. 7
vols. Heinemann, 1927–43. (Harvard
UP, 1927–43)

[5]JUVENAL 'Satire VI' in *Works* trans
G. G. Ramsay 1918. op. (Harvard
UP, 1920)

[6]PLINY the younger *Letters of the
younger Pliny* trans B. Radice.
Penguin, 1963

[7]*Beowulf* trans M. Alexander. Penguin,
1973

[8]There would have been beds on both
ground and first floors of modest hall
houses and two storey cottages. In
Chaucer's 'Miller's Tale', from *The
Canterbury Tales*, the aged carpenter
and his lascivious young wife share a
bed on the ground floor while the
lecherous lodger lives on the first
floor. The location of the master's bed
on the ground floor was probably
usual and good for security.

[9]CHAUCER, G. *The Canterbury tales*
trans N. Coghill, Penguin, 1951. op.
(Penguin, 1978)

[10]LANGLAND, W. *Piers the ploughman*
trans J. F. Goodridge. Penguin, 1959.
op. (Penguin, 1970)

[11]*Sir Gawain and the green knight* trans B.
Stone. Penguin, 1959. op. (Penguin,
1970)

[12]British Museum, Dept of Manuscripts.
Harleian 6815, ff 22–38v

[13]PARKER, R. *The common stream*
Collins, 1975. op. (Paladin, 1976)

[14]PEPYS, S. *Diary of Samuel Pepys* eds.
R. Latham and W. Matthews. 11
vols. Bell, 1970–83. op.

[15]ibid, entry for 9 October, 1667

[16]WOTTON, H. *The elements of
architecture, collected from the best
authors* Longman, 1903. op. (Gregg
International, 1969)

[17]FIENNES, C. Through England on a
side saddle in the time of William and
Mary: the diary of Celia Fiennes ed.
Mrs Griffiths. Field and Tuer, 1888.
op.
The great chamber's occasional role
as a state dining room is confirmed
in Celia Fiennes informative
description of the Chatsworth state
apartments as they appeared a few
years after their completion in 1695.
From the lofty hall she ascended to
'the dining roome, two drawing
rooms, a bed chamber and closet
which open quite thro' the house a
visto, and at the End of the dining
room is a large door all of looking
glass in great pannells all diamond
cutt. This is just opposite to ye doores
that runs into ye drawing roome and
bed chamber and closet so it shews
ye rooms to look all double.' (Written
in May 1667.)

[18]The arrangement at Blenheim Palace
(1705–16) is revealing. The pair of
state apartments—each consisting of
four rooms aligned each side of the
central saloon—both contained a state
bedchamber. The convention was

that King and Queen, when visiting, should be seen to keep separate establishments with individual bed-chambers, as befitted their status and grandeur. This was hardly a necessary arrangement in the early eighteenth century of Queen Anne.

The state rooms were separated by five large public rooms, so movement between them would have been most conspicuous. By contrast the Duke and Duchess of Marlborough, in their private apartment, possessed bedchambers separated by only two rooms.

[19] EVELYN, J. *Diary of John Evelyn* ed. W. Bray. Dent, 1966. op.

[20] CHESTERFIELD, 4th Earl *Characters of eminent personages of his time* by Lord Chesterfield. 1777. op.

[21] BOSWELL, J. *Life of Johnson* ed. A. Birrell. Vol 2. Constable, 1986

[22] NORTH, R. *Of building: writings on architecture* ed. H. Colvin and J. Newman. OUP, 1981

[23] VANBRUGH, J. *Completed works of Sir John Vanbrugh* ed. B. Bubree and G. Webb. Vol 4: *Letters*. Nonesuch Press, 1927–29. op.

[24] See [22]

[25] EDEN, W. A and WRAGG, R. B. *John Carr: stonecutter extraordinary* Transactions of the Ancient Monuments Society. NS24, 1980

[26] HERVEY OF ICKWORTH, Baron *Lord Hervey and his friends* ed. Earl of Ilchester. Murray, 1950. op.

[27] GANDON and WOOLFE *Vitruvius Britannicus* Plan of Holkham Hall (*piano nobile* level), 1771. op.

[28] See [14] entry of 28 December, 1664. Pepys reveals that on waking in the night he 'lacked a pot ... and bitter cold, so was forced to rise and piss in the chimney.'

[29] KETTON-CREMER, R. W. *Felbrigg: the history of a house* Hart-Davis, 1962. op. (Century, 1986)

[30] See [17]

[31] Quoted in LAMBTON, L. *Temples of convenience* Gordon Fraser Gallery, 1978. op.

[32] See [14] entry for 15 May, 1667. Sweating in a hot bath was believed

to be a beneficial treatment for syphilis. Pepys includes in this entry: 'Mr Lowden is come to use the Tubb; that is to bathe and sweat himself, and that his Lady is come to use the Tubb too; which (we) take to be that he hath and hath given her the pox'.

[33] See [14] entry for 29 May, 1664. This entry includes a description of Mr Povy's house: 'after dinner, up and down to see his house (on the south side of Lincoln's Inn Fields). And in a word, methink for his perspective upon the wall of his garden (a *trompel'œil* by Richard Streeter), and the Spring's riseing up—with the perspective in the little closet—his room floored above with woods of several colours, like, but above the best cabinet work I ever saw—his grotto and vault, with his bottles of wine and a well therein to keep them cool, his furniture of all sorts—his bath at the top of his house—good pictures and his manner of eating and drinking, doth surpass all ever I did see of one man in my life.'

[34] See [14] entry for 10 October, 1667

[35] The appearance of a London bed-chamber of a couple of generations earlier can be pieced together from Pepys's description of his bed chamber in Seething Lane. The walls were hung with red fabric, as was the bed (in 1663) and was later (1666) rehung with blue fabric, with the red being reused in Pepys's dressing room.

[36] WARE, I. *A complete body of architecture, adorned with plans and elevations from original designs* T. Osborne and J. Shipton, 1756. op. (Gregg International, 1971.)

[37] BRONTË, E. *Wuthering heights* Many edns., including Penguin, 1990

[38] PECCHIO, Count *Semi-serious observations of an Italian exile during his residence in England* London, 1833. op.

[39] See [14] entry for November, 1662. This entry concludes thus: 'at night to supper and bed this night having first put up a spitting-sheet, which I find very convenient.'

[40] See [14] entry for 20 October, 1660.

Three years later Pepys was still having trouble with Mr Turner: 'down to my cellar, and up and down with Mr Turner to see where his vault for Turds may be made bigger, or another made him.' (entry for 8 July, 1663)

Pepys also throws considerable light on the working methods of night soil men: 'thence home, where my house of office was emptying, and I find they will do it with much more cleanliness than I expected ... up about 6 a'clock, and I find the people have just gone.' The memory of the process proved too much for Pepys, for that evening he had to dine with neighbours, 'having no stomach to dine at home, it being hardly clear of last night's turds.' (28/29 July, 1663)

[41] SWIFT, J. *A panegyric of the Reverend Dean Swift* Dublin, 1729–30; London, 1710. op.

[42] CRUICKSHANK, D. and BURTON, N. *Life in the Georgian city* Viking, 1990. This practice explains why even fashionable houses in the West End of London possessed few lavatories until the very end of the eighteenth century. For example, 11 Queen Anne's Gate, St James's, built in 1771, contained one lavatory in the yard and another in the pavement vault, reached via the kitchen and basement area.

[43] SIMOND, L. *An American in Regency England: journal of a tour and residence in Great Britain during the years 1810 and 1811, by a French traveller* ed. C. Hibbert. R. Maxwell, 1968. op.

[44] NICHOLSON, P. *New practical builder* 1823–25. op. As late as the 1770s Robert Adam's great aristocratic town houses—such as 20 St James's Square (1771) and Derby House, Grosvenor Square (1773)—still only had lavatories, albeit water closets, in the private family apartments. Presumably, these were available for guests at parties, or else a room must have been provided with close-stools. The plans for 28 Soho Square, London (1774)

are more advanced for they show a 'servant's privy' in a pavement vault, a water closet adjoining the ground floor dressing room and accessible for guests because it was reached from the yard, as well as another water closet off the first floor rear bedroom. (See [42].) By the 1820s even modest houses in great cities had at least one internal water closet, as revealed by the four different 'rates' of terrace houses published by Nicholson.

[45]Quoted in STONE, L. *The family, sex and marriage in England 1500–1800* Penguin, 1979. (Penguin, 1990)

[46]See [14] entry for 3 October, 1663. Pepys records the type of bell arrangement usual before the introduction of the wire operated remote system: '... well pleased with my new lodgings and the convenience of having our maids and no one else about us ... abroad to buy a bell to hang by our chamber door to call the maids.'

[47]SOUTHEY, R. *Letters from England by Don Manuel Alvarez Espriella* A. Sutton, 1984. op.
In these letters Southey, using the pseudonym of Don Manuel Alvarez Espriella, and writing in 1807, gives an excellent description of an early nineteenth century bedroom as a place of privacy, repose and reflection: 'my bed, though neither covered with silk nor satin, has as much ornament as is suitable—linen curtains hang in folds round the bed posts, which are light pillars of mahogany. My window curtains are of the same pattern as the bed; a mohogany press holds my clothes; an oval looking-glass swinging lengthways stands on the dressing table; a compact kind of chest holds the basin, the soap, the tooth brush, and water glass, each in a separate compartment; and a looking-glass, for the purpose of shaving at ... slips up and down behind. The water jug and water bottle stand below ... the room is carpeted; here I have my fire, my table, and my cassette.'

[48]Quoted in: SAMPSON, H. *A history of advertising* London, 1874. op.

[49]Quoted in WRIGHT, L. *Clean and decent* Routledge, 1960, 1966; r.e., 1980. op.

[50]Lanhydrock House, Devon, designed in 1881, possesses a self-contained nursery suite complete with its own guest nursery for visiting children.

[51]MUTHESIUS, H. *Das Englische Haus* Berlin, 1904–5. Also published in English as *The English house* Crosby, Lockwood, Staples, 1979. op.

[52]ROBERTS, H. *Dwellings of the labouring classes* London, r.e. 1867. op.

[53]HARRIS, E. *Going to bed* HMSO, 1981. op. and STOPES, M. C. *Sleep* Chatto, 1956. op.

[54]HENLEY CENTRE FOR FORECASTING *Planning for social change* Henley Centre for Forecasting, 1986. op.

CHAPTER THREE

[1]Pope quoted in: *Harcourt Papers* ed. E. W. Harcourt, 14 vols. Oxford, 1880–1905 (50 copies printed for private circulation; one copy in British Library)

[2]WEIGHTMAN, G. and HUMPHRIES, S. *The making of modern London 1914–1939* Sidgwick & Jackson, 1984. op.

[3]Mrs Gaskell quoted in: COOK, O. *English cottages and farmhouses* Thames & Hudson, new edn., 1985

[4]HOLLAND, Lady S. *A memoir of the Reverend Sydney Smith ... with a selection from his letters* 2 vols. London, 1855

[5]BEETON, Mrs I. *Book of household management* Cape, 1968. (New impression of 1861 edition)

[6]GIROUARD, M. *The Victorian country house* OUP, 1971; Yale UP; pb. 1985

[7]CRUICKSHANK, D. and BURTON, N. *Life in the Georgian city* Viking, 1990

[8]WORSDALL, F. *Glasgow tenement – a way of life* Chambers, new edn., 1991

[9]Mrs Lancaster quoted in: DAVIDSON, C. *A woman's work is never done* Chatto & Windus, 1982. op. This work was used in the general research for this chapter, and serves as useful background reading on the subject of the kitchen in the history of the British home.

[10]PEARSON, L. F. *The architectural and social history of cooperative living* Macmillan, 1988

[11]MUTHESIUS, H. *Das Englische Haus* Berlin, 1904–5. First published in English as *The English House* Crosby, Lockwood, Staples, 1979. op.

[12]*Making space: women and the man-made environment* Pluto, 1984

[13]See [9]

[14]*Daily Express home of today* Many edns., including Daily Express, nd

[15]BURNETT, J. *A short history of housing 1815-1970* Methuen, rev. edn., 1986

[16]See [9]

CHAPTER FOUR

In addition to innumerable press cuttings, magazine and newspaper articles, press advertisements and TV commercials studied—the most important of which are cited both in the text and below—the following documents were also of great assistance in compiling this chapter of the book:

[1]THOMPSON, M. *Rubbish theory: the creation and destruction of value* OUP, 1079. op.

[2]COWBURN, W. 'Popular housing'. *Arena: the journal of the Architectural Association*, October, 1966

[3]ADAM, R. 'Tin gods and contemporary architecture' *The recent works of Robert Adam* Published privately, 1990

Housing finance into the 1990s Building Societies Association, 1985

MUELLBAUER, J. The dream house effect *Roof*, May/June 1990

PAWLEY, M. *Home ownership* Architectural Press, 1978. op.

PAWLEY, M. *The private future: causes and consequences of community collapse in the west* Thames & Hudson, 1974.

Social trends 16 Central Statistical Office, 1986

INDEX